INFORMATION SYSTEMS AND CYBERSECURITY CAPSTONE PROJECT

Request for Proposals for Information Security Assessment Services (ISAS)

JONES & BARTLETT
LEARNING

World Headquarters
Jones & Bartlett Learning
5 Wall Street
Burlington, MA 01803
978-443-5000
info@jblearning.com
www.jblearning.com

Jones & Bartlett Learning books and products are available through most bookstores and online booksellers. To contact Jones & Bartlett Learning directly, call 800-832-0034, fax 978-443-8000, or visit our website, www.jblearning.com.

This publication is designed to provide accurate and authoritative information in regard to the subject matter covered. It is sold with the understanding that the publisher is not engaged in rendering legal, accounting, or other professional service. If legal advice or other expert assistance is required, the service of a competent professional person should be sought.

Production Credits
Chief Executive Officer: Ty Field
President: James Homer
SVP, Editor-in-Chief: Michael Johnson
SVP, Chief Marketing Officer: Alison M. Pendergast
SVP, Curriculum Solutions: Christopher Will
Authors: Michael G. Solomon, David Kim
Editorial Management: High Stakes Writing, LLC; Lawrence J. Goodrich, Editor and Publisher
Production Editor: Tina Chen
Senior Marketing Manager: Andrea DeFronzo
Manufacturing and Inventory Control Supervisor: Amy Bacus
Cover Design: Kristin Parker
Composition: High Stakes Writing
Cover Image: © ErickN/ShutterStock, Inc.
Printing and Binding: Malloy, Inc.
Cover Printing: Malloy, Inc.

ISBN: 978-1-4496-7118-1

6048
Printed in the United States of America
16 15 14 13 12   10 9 8 7 6 5 4 3 2 1

STATE GOVERNMENT
DEPARTMENT OF FINANCE AND ADMINISTRATION

REQUEST FOR PROPOSALS
FOR
INFORMATION SECURITY ASSESSMENT SERVICES (ISAS)
RFP NUMBER: 427.04-107-08

CONTENTS

1 INTRODUCTION

1.1 Statement of Purpose

The State Government, Department of Finance and Administration, hereinafter referred to as the State, has issued this Request for Proposals (RFP) to define the State's minimum service requirements; solicit proposals; detail proposal requirements; and outline the State's process for evaluating proposals and selecting the contractor.

Through this RFP, the State seeks to buy the best services at the most favorable, competitive prices and to give ALL qualified businesses, including those that are owned by minorities, women, persons with a disability, and small business enterprises, opportunity to do business with the state as contractors and subcontractors.

The State intends to secure a contract for Information Security Assessment Services (ISAS) Consultants to assist in strengthening the State's security posture. Services include vulnerability assessments, penetration tests, and source code reviews. Vulnerability assessments and penetration testing services will be used to identify and validate configuration and/or technical flaws within a given system or network (i.e. firewalls, routers, servers, operating systems, applications, databases, load balancers, etc.). Source code reviews will be conducted to identify programming errors that may lead to security issues (i.e. format string mistakes, buffer overflows, memory leaks, etc.).

A vendor that currently has active managed-security service provider contract(s) with any State Government agency **cannot** bid on this RFP. In addition, during the term of the Contract awarded from this RFP, the winning vendor **cannot** bid on any procurement for managed-security services released by State Government agencies or otherwise provide managed-security services to State Government agencies.

The vendor shall provide the services required by this RFP within the context of the technical environment described by the *State Information Resources Architecture* (sometimes referred to as the technical architecture). The vendor may request a copy of the Architecture by submitting a written request to the RFP coordinator listed in RFP Section 1.5.1.1.

1.2 Scope of Service, Contract Period, and Required Terms and Conditions

The RFP Attachment 6.1, *Pro Forma* Contract details the State's required:

- Scope of Services and Deliverables in Section A
- Contract Period in Section B
- Payment Terms in Section C
- Standard Terms and Conditions in Section D
- Special Terms and Conditions in Section E

The *pro forma* contract substantially represents the contract document that the proposer selected by the State MUST agree to and sign.

1.3 Nondiscrimination

No person shall be excluded from participation in, be denied benefits of, be discriminated against in the admission or access to, or be discriminated against in treatment or employment in the State's contracted programs or activities on the grounds of disability, age, race, color, religion, sex, national origin, or any other classification protected by federal or State Constitutional or statutory law; nor shall any person be excluded from participation in, be denied benefits of, or be otherwise subjected to discrimination in the performance of contracts with the State or in the employment practices of the State's contractors. Accordingly, all vendors entering into contracts with the State shall, upon request, be required to show proof of such nondiscrimination and to post in conspicuous places, available to all employees and applicants, notices of nondiscrimination.

The State has designated the following to coordinate compliance with the nondiscrimination requirements of the State Government, Title VI of the Civil Rights Act of 1964, the Americans with Disabilities Act of 1990, and applicable federal regulations.

Jane Doe, PhD
Senior Management Consultant
F&A / Office of Consulting Services

State Government Tower
100 1st Avenue
Capitol City, NY 12345-1200
Ph: 866-555-1212

1.4   **Assistance to Proposers With a Disability**

A Proposer with a disability may receive accommodation regarding the means of communicating this RFP and participating in this RFP process. A Proposer with a disability should contact the RFP Coordinator to request reasonable accommodation no later than the Disability Accommodation Request Deadline detailed in the RFP Section 2, Schedule of Events.

1.5   **RFP Communications**

1.5.1   **Unauthorized contact regarding this RFP with employees or officials of the State Government other than the RFP Coordinator detailed below may result in disqualification from this procurement process.**

1.5.1.1   Interested Parties must direct all communications regarding this RFP to the following RFP Coordinator, who is the state Government's only official point of contact for this RFP.

> John Doe
> Department of Finance and Administration
> State Government Tower
> 100 1st Avenue
> Capitol City, NY 12345-1200
> Ph: 866-555-1212
> Fax: 866-555-1213
> John.Doe@state.ny.us

1.5.1.2   Notwithstanding the foregoing, Interested Parties may contact the staff of the Governor's Office of Diversity Business Enterprise for general public information regarding this RFP, assistance available from the Governor's Office of Diversity Business Enterprise, or potential future state procurements.

1.5.2   The State has assigned the following RFP identification number that must be referenced in all communications regarding the RFP:

RFP-427.04-107-08

1.5.3   Any oral communications shall be considered unofficial and non-binding with regard to this RFP.

1.5.4   Each Proposer shall assume the risk of the method of dispatching any communication or proposal to the State. The State assumes no responsibility for delays or delivery failures resulting from the method of dispatch. Actual or electronic "postmarking" of a communication or proposal to the State by a deadline date shall <u>not</u> substitute for actual receipt of a communication or proposal by the State.

1.5.5   The RFP Coordinator <u>must</u> receive all written comments, including questions and requests for clarification, no later than the Written Comments Deadline detailed in the RFP Section 2, Schedule of Events.

1.5.6   The State reserves the right to determine, at its sole discretion, the appropriate and adequate responses to written comments, questions, and requests for clarification. The State's official responses and other official communications pursuant to this RFP shall constitute an amendment of this RFP.

1.5.7   The State will convey all official responses and communications pursuant to this RFP to the potential proposers from whom the State has received a Notice of Intent to Propose.

1.5.8   Only the State's official, written responses and communications shall be considered binding with regard to this RFP.

1.5.9   The State reserves the right to determine, at its sole discretion, the method of conveying official responses and communications pursuant to this RFP (*e.g.*, written, facsimile, electronic mail, or Internet posting). Most important documents will be posted on the State's website.

1.5.10   Any data or factual information provided by the State, in this RFP or an official response or communication, shall be deemed for informational purposes only, and if a Proposer relies on such data or factual information, the Proposer should either: (1) independently verify the information or (2) obtain the State's written consent to rely thereon.

1.6   Notice of Intent to Propose

Each potential Proposer should submit a Notice of Intent to Propose to the RFP Coordinator by the deadline detailed in the RFP Section 2, Schedule of Events. The notice should include:

- Proposer's name
- name and title of a contact person
- address, telephone number, and facsimile number of the contact person
- email address

NOTICE: A Notice of Intent to Propose creates no obligation and is not a prerequisite for making a proposal; however, it is necessary to ensure receipt of RFP amendments and other communications regarding the RFP (refer to RFP Sections 1.5, *et seq.*, above).

1.7   Proposal Deadline

Proposals must be submitted no later than the Proposal Deadline time and date detailed in the RFP Section 2, Schedule of Events. A proposal must respond to the written RFP and any RFP exhibits, attachments, or amendments. A late proposal shall not be accepted, and a Proposer's failure to submit a proposal before the deadline shall cause the proposal to be disqualified.

1.8   Pre-Proposal Conference

A Pre-Proposal Conference will be held at the time and date detailed in the RFP Section 2, Schedule of Events. The purpose of the conference is to discuss the RFP scope of services. While questions will be entertained, the response to any question at the Pre-Proposal Conference shall be considered tentative and non-binding with regard to this RFP. Questions concerning the RFP should be submitted in writing prior to the Written Comments Deadline date detailed in the RFP Section 2, Schedule of Events. To ensure accurate, consistent responses to all known potential Proposers, the official response to questions will be issued by the State as described in RFP Sections 1.5, *et seq.*, above and on the date detailed in the RFP Section 2, Schedule of Events.

Pre-Proposal Conference attendance is <u>not</u> mandatory, and each potential Proposer may be limited to a maximum number of attendees depending upon overall attendance and space limitations. The conference will be held at:

Auditorium
State Government Tower
100 1st Avenue
Capitol City, NY 12345-1200
Ph: 866-555-1212

2　RFP SCHEDULE OF EVENTS

The following Schedule of Events represents the State's best estimate of the schedule that will be followed. Unless otherwise specified, the time of day for the following events will be between 8:00 a.m. and 4:30 p.m., Eastern Time.

RFP SCHEDULE OF EVENTS

NOTICE: The State reserves the right, at its sole discretion, to adjust this schedule as it deems necessary. The State will communicate any adjustment to the Schedule of Events to the potential Proposers from whom the State has received a Notice of Intent to Propose.

EVENT	TIME	DATE (all dates are state business days)
1. State Issues RFP		
2. Disability Accommodation Request Deadline		
3. Pre-Proposal Conference	10:00 a.m.	
4. Notice of Intent to Propose Deadline		
5. Written Comments Deadline		
6. State Responds to Written Comments		
7. Proposal Deadline		
8. State Completes Technical Proposal Evaluations		
9. State Opens Cost Proposals and Calculates Scores		
10. State Issues Evaluation Notice and Opens RFP Files for Public Inspection		
11. Contract Signing		
12. Contract Signature Deadline		
13. Contract Start Date		

3   PROPOSAL REQUIREMENTS

Each Proposer must submit a proposal in response to this RFP with the most favorable terms that the Proposer can offer. There will be no best and final offer procedure.

3.1   Proposal Form and Delivery

3.1.1   Each response to this RFP must consist of a Technical Proposal and a Cost Proposal (as described below).

3.1.2   Each Proposer must submit one (1) original and six (6) copies, and one (1) CD containing a copy in ".pdf" format of the Technical Proposal to the State in a sealed package that is clearly marked:

"Technical Proposal in Response to RFP- 427.04-107-08 -- Do Not Open"

NOTE: One hard copy must be marked "Original." In the event of any differences between printed and electronic versions, or problems with the CD, the contents of the hard copy marked "Original" shall prevail. Do not include any costs in either form of the Technical Proposal.

3.1.3   Each Proposer must submit one (1) Cost Proposal to the State in a separate, sealed package that is clearly marked:

"Cost Proposal in Response to RFP- 427.04-107-08 -- Do Not Open"

3.1.4   If a Proposer encloses the separately sealed proposals (as detailed above) in a larger package for mailing, the Proposer must clearly mark the outermost package:

"Contains Separately Sealed Technical and Cost Proposals for RFP # 427.04-107-08"

3.1.5   The State must receive all proposals in response to this RFP, at the following address, no later than the Proposal Deadline time and date detailed in the RFP Section 2, Schedule of Events.

> John Doe
> Department of Finance and Administration
> State Government Tower
> 100 1st Avenue
> Capitol City, NY 12345-1200
> Ph: 866-555-1212
> Fax: 866-555-1213

3.1.6   A Proposer may not deliver a proposal orally or by any means of electronic transmission.

3.2   Technical Proposal

3.2.1   The RFP Attachment 6.3, Technical Proposal and Evaluation Guide, details specific requirements for making a Technical Proposal in response to this RFP. This guide includes mandatory and general requirements as well as technical queries requiring a written response.

NOTICE: No pricing information shall be included in the Technical Proposal. Inclusion of Cost Proposal amounts in the Technical Proposal shall make the proposal non-responsive and the State shall reject it.

3.2.2   Each Proposer must use the Technical Proposal and Evaluation Guide to organize, reference, and draft the Technical Proposal. Each Proposer should duplicate the Technical Proposal and Evaluation Guide and use it as a table of contents covering the Technical Proposal (adding proposal page numbers as appropriate).

3.2.3   Each proposal should be economically prepared, with emphasis on completeness and clarity of content. A proposal, as well as any reference material presented, must be written in English and must be written on standard 8 1/2" x 11" paper (although foldouts containing charts, spreadsheets, and oversize exhibits are permissible). All proposal pages must be numbered.

3.2.4   All information included in a Technical Proposal should be relevant to a specific requirement detailed in the Technical Proposal and Evaluation Guide. All information must be incorporated into a response to a specific requirement and clearly referenced. Any information not meeting these criteria will be deemed extraneous and will in no way contribute to the evaluation process.

3.2.5   The State may determine a proposal to be non-responsive and reject it if the Proposer fails to organize and properly reference the Technical Proposal as required by this RFP and the Technical Proposal and Evaluation Guide.

3.2.6   The State may determine a proposal to be non-responsive and reject it if the Technical Proposal document fails to appropriately address/meet all of the requirements detailed in the Technical Proposal and Evaluation Guide.

3.3   Cost Proposal

3.3.1   The Cost Proposal <u>must</u> be submitted to the State in a <u>sealed</u> package separate from the Technical proposal.

3.3.2   Each Cost Proposal <u>must</u> be recorded on an exact duplicate of the RFP Attachment 6.4, Cost Proposal and Evaluation Guide.

3.3.3   <u>Each Proposer shall ONLY record the proposed cost exactly as required by the Cost Proposal and Evaluation Guide and shall NOT record any other rates, amounts, or information.</u>

3.3.4   The proposed cost shall incorporate <u>all</u> costs for services under the contract for the total contract period.

3.3.5.   The Proposer must sign and date the Cost Proposal.

3.3.6   If a Proposer fails to submit a Cost Proposal as required, the State shall determine the proposal to be non-responsive and reject it.

4   GENERAL REQUIREMENTS & CONTRACTING INFORMATION

4.1   Proposer Required Review and Waiver of Objections

Each Proposer must carefully review this RFP and all attachments, including but not limited to the *pro forma* contract, for comments, questions, defects, objections, or any other matter requiring clarification or correction (collectively called "comments"). Comments concerning RFP objections must be made in writing and received by the State no later than the Written Comments Deadline detailed in the RFP Section 2, Schedule of Events. This will allow issuance of any necessary amendments and help prevent the opening of defective proposals upon which contract award could not be made.

Protests based on any objection shall be considered waived and invalid if these comments/objections have not been brought to the attention of the State, in writing, by the Written Comments Deadline.

4.2   RFP Amendment and Cancellation

The State reserves the unilateral right to amend this RFP in writing at any time. If an RFP amendment is issued, the State will convey such amendment to the potential Proposers who submitted a Notice of Intent to Propose. Each proposal must respond to the final written RFP and any exhibits, attachments, and amendments.

The State Government reserves the right, at its sole discretion, to cancel and reissue this RFP or to cancel this RFP in its entirety in accordance with applicable laws and regulations.

4.3   Proposal Prohibitions and Right of Rejection

4.3.1   The State Government reserves the right, at its sole discretion, to reject any and all proposals in accordance with applicable laws and regulations.

4.3.2   Each proposal must comply with all of the terms of this RFP and all applicable State laws and regulations. The State may reject any proposal that does not comply with all of the terms, conditions, and performance requirements of this RFP. The State may consider any proposal that does not meet the requirements of this RFP to be non-responsive, and the State may reject such a proposal.

4.3.3   A proposal of alternate services (*i.e.*, a proposal that offers services different from those requested by this RFP) shall be considered non-responsive and rejected.

4.3.4   A Proposer may not restrict the rights of the State or otherwise qualify a proposal. The State may determine such a proposal to be a non-responsive counteroffer, and the proposal may be rejected.

4.3.5   A Proposer may not submit the Proposer's own contract terms and conditions in a response to this RFP. If a proposal contains such terms and conditions, the State may determine, at its sole discretion, the proposal to be a non-responsive counteroffer, and the proposal may be rejected.

4.3.6   A Proposer shall not submit more than one proposal. Submitting more than one proposal shall result in the disqualification of the Proposer.

4.3.7   A Proposer shall not submit multiple proposals in different forms. This prohibited action shall be defined as a Proposer submitting one proposal as a prime contractor and permitting a second Proposer to submit another proposal with the first Proposer offered as a subcontractor. This restriction does not prohibit different Proposers from offering the same subcontractor as a part of their proposals, provided that the subcontractor does not also submit a proposal as a prime contractor. Submitting multiple proposals in different forms may result in the disqualification of all Proposers knowingly involved.

4.3.8   The State shall reject a proposal if the Cost Proposal was not arrived at independently without collusion, consultation, communication, or agreement as to any matter relating to such prices with any other Proposer. Regardless of the time of detection, the State shall consider any of the foregoing prohibited actions to be grounds for proposal rejection or contract termination.

4.3.9   The State shall <u>not</u> contract with or consider a proposal from:

4.3.9.1   an individual who is, or within the past six months has been, an employee or official of the State Government;

4.3.9.2   a company, corporation, or any other contracting entity in which an ownership of two percent (2%) or more is held by an individual who is, or within the past six months has been, an employee or official of the State Government (this shall not apply either to financial interests that have been placed into a "blind trust" arrangement pursuant to which the employee does not have knowledge of the retention or disposition of such interests or to the ownership of publicly traded stocks or bonds where such ownership constitutes less than 2% of the total outstanding amount of the stocks or bonds of the issuing entity);

4.3.9.3   a company, corporation, or any other contracting entity which employs an individual who is, or within the past six months has been, an employee or official of the State Government in a position that would allow the direct or indirect use or disclosure of information, which was obtained through or in connection with his or her employment and not made available to the general public, for the purpose of furthering the private interest or personal profit of any person; or,

4.3.9.4   any individual, company, or other entity involved in assisting the State in the development, formulation, or drafting of this RFP or its scope of services shall be considered to have been given information that would afford an unfair advantage over other Proposers, and such individual, company, or other entity may not submit a proposal in response to this RFP.

4.3.9.5   For the purposes of applying the requirements of RFP subsection 4.3.9, *et. seq.*, an individual shall be deemed an employee or official of the State Government until such time as all compensation for salary, termination pay, and annual leave has been paid.

4.3.10   The State reserves the right, at its sole discretion, to waive a proposal's variances from full compliance with this RFP. If the State waives minor variances in a proposal, such waiver shall not modify the RFP requirements or excuse the Proposer from full compliance with such. Notwithstanding any minor variance, the State may hold any Proposer to strict compliance with this RFP.

4.4   Incorrect Proposal Information

If the State determines that a Proposer has provided, for consideration in this RFP process or subsequent contract negotiations, incorrect information that the Proposer knew or should have known was materially incorrect, that proposal shall be determined non-responsive and shall be rejected.

4.5   Proposal of Additional Services

If a proposal offers services in addition to those required by and described in this RFP, the additional services may be added to the contract before contract signing at the sole discretion of the State. Notwithstanding the foregoing, a Proposer shall not propose any additional cost amount(s) or rate(s) for additional services.

NOTICE: The Proposer's Cost Proposal shall record only the proposed cost as required in this RFP and shall not record any other rates, amounts, or information. If a Proposer fails to submit a Cost Proposal as required, the State shall determine the proposal to be non-responsive and shall reject the proposal.

4.6   Assignment and Subcontracting

4.6.1   The Proposer awarded a contract pursuant to this RFP may not subcontract, transfer, or assign any portion of the contract without the State's prior, written approval.

4.6.2   A subcontractor may be substituted for a proposed subcontractor only at the discretion of the State and with the State's prior written approval.

4.6.3   At its sole discretion, the State reserves the right to refuse approval of any subcontract, transfer, or assignment.

4.6.4   Notwithstanding State approval of each subcontractor, the Proposer, if awarded a contract pursuant to this RFP, shall be the prime contractor and shall be responsible for all work performed.

4.7   Right to Refuse Personnel

At its sole discretion, the State reserves the right to refuse any personnel, of the prime contractor or a subcontractor, for use in the performance of a contract pursuant to this RFP.

4.8   Insurance

The State may require the apparent successful Proposer to provide proof of adequate worker's compensation and public liability insurance coverage before entering into a contract. Additionally, the

State may require, at its sole discretion, the apparent successful Proposer to provide proof of adequate professional malpractice liability or other forms of insurance. Failure to provide evidence of such insurance coverage is a material breach and grounds for termination of the contract negotiations. Any insurance required by the State shall be in form and substance acceptable to the State.

4.9   Licensure

Before a contract pursuant to this RFP is signed, the apparent successful Proposer must hold all necessary, applicable business and professional licenses. The State may require any or all Proposers to submit evidence of proper licensure.

4.10   Service Location and Work Space

The service pursuant to this RFP is to be performed, completed, managed, and delivered as detailed in the RFP Attachment 6.1, *Pro Forma* Contract. Work space on the State's premises may be available for contractor use in accordance with the *pro forma* contract or at the State's discretion.

4.11   Proposal Withdrawal

A Proposer may withdraw a submitted proposal at any time up to the Proposal Deadline time and date detailed in the RFP Section 2, Schedule of Events. To do so, a proposer must submit a written request, signed by a Proposer's authorized representative to withdraw a proposal. After withdrawing a previously submitted proposal, a Proposer may submit another proposal at any time up to the Proposal Deadline.

4.12   Proposal Errors and Amendments

Each Proposer is liable for all proposal errors or omissions. A Proposer will not be allowed to alter or amend proposal documents after the Proposal Deadline time and date detailed in the RFP Section 2, Schedule of Events, unless such is formally requested, in writing, by the State.

4.13   Proposal Preparation Costs

The State will not pay any costs associated with the preparation, submittal, or presentation of any proposal.

4.14   Disclosure of Proposal Contents

Each proposal and all materials submitted to the State in response to this RFP shall become the property of the State Government. Selection or rejection of a proposal does not affect this right. All proposal information, including detailed price and cost information, shall be held in confidence during the evaluation process. Notwithstanding, a list of actual proposers submitting timely proposals may be available to the public, upon request, directly after technical proposals are opened by the state.

Upon the completion of the evaluation of proposals, indicated by public release of an Evaluation Notice, the proposals and associated materials shall be open for review by the public in accordance with *State Code Annotated*, Section 10-7-504(a)(7). By submitting a proposal, the Proposer acknowledges and accepts that the full proposal contents and associated documents shall become open to public inspection.

4.15   Contractor Registration

While registration with the State is <u>not</u> required to make a proposal, a service provider must be registered to do business with the State Government before approval of an awarded contract. To meet this prerequisite, an unregistered service provider must simply register as required prior to contract approval. Fast and easy access to *Online Contractor Registration* is available at the State's website.

(For more information about registration, please contact the Department of General Services)

4.16   Contract Approval

The RFP and the contractor selection processes do not obligate the State and do not create rights, interests, or claims of entitlement in either the Proposer with the apparent best-evaluated proposal or any other Proposer. Contract award and State obligations pursuant thereto shall commence only after the contract is signed by the Contractor and the head of the procuring state agency and after the contract is approved and signed by all other State officials as required by State laws and regulations.

4.17 Contract Payments

All contract payments shall be made in accordance with the contract's Payment Terms and Conditions provisions (refer to RFP Attachment 6.1, *Pro Forma* Contract, Section C). No payment shall be made until the contract is approved as required by State laws and regulations. Under no conditions shall the State be liable for payment of any type associated with the contract or responsible for any work done by the Contractor, even work done in good faith and even if the Contractor is orally directed to proceed with the delivery of services, if it occurs before contract approval by State officials as required by applicable statutes and rules of the State Government or before the contract start date or after the contract end date specified by the contract.

4.18 Contractor Performance

The Contractor shall be responsible for the completion of all work set out in the contract. All work is subject to inspection, evaluation, and acceptance by the State. The State may employ all reasonable means to ensure that the work is progressing and being performed in compliance with the contract. At reasonable times, the State may inspect those areas of the Contractor's place of business that are related to the performance of the contract. If the State requires such an inspection, the Contractor shall provide reasonable access and assistance.

4.19 Contract Amendment

During the course of this contract, the State may request the Contractor to perform additional work for which the Contractor would be compensated. That work shall be within the general scope of this RFP. In such instances, the State shall provide the Contractor a written description of the additional work, and the Contractor shall submit a time schedule for accomplishing the additional work and a price for the additional work based on the rates included in the Contractor's proposal to this RFP. If the State and the Contractor reach an agreement regarding the work and associated compensation, such agreement shall be effected by means of a contract amendment. Any such amendment requiring additional work must be mutually agreed upon by the parties and signed by the Contractor and the head of the procuring state agency and must be approved by other State officials as required by State laws and regulations. The Contractor shall not commence additional work until the State has issued a written contract amendment and secured all required approvals.

4.20 Severability

If any provision of this RFP is declared by a court to be illegal or in conflict with any law, said decision shall not affect the validity of the remaining RFP terms and provisions, and the rights and obligations of the State and Proposers shall be construed and enforced as if the RFP did not contain the particular provision held to be invalid.

5   PROPOSAL EVALUATION & CONTRACT AWARD

5.1   Evaluation Categories and Maximum Points

The State will consider qualifications and experience, technical approach, technical requirements, and cost in the evaluation of proposals. The maximum points that shall be awarded for each of these categories are detailed below.

CATEGORY	MAXIMUM POINTS POSSIBLE
Qualifications and Experience	30
Technical Approach	40
Cost Proposal	30

5.2   Evaluation Process

The proposal evaluation process is designed to award the contract not necessarily to the Proposer of least cost, but rather to the Proposer with the best combination of attributes based upon the evaluation criteria.

5.2.1   The RFP Coordinator will use the RFP Attachment 6.3, Technical Proposal and Evaluation Guide to manage the Technical Proposal Evaluation and maintain evaluation records.

5.2.1.1   The RFP Coordinator will review each Technical Proposal to determine compliance with mandatory requirements (refer to RFP Attachment 6.3, Technical Proposal and Evaluation Guide, Technical Proposal Section A). If the RFP Coordinator determines that a proposal may have failed to meet one or more of the mandatory requirements, the Proposal Evaluation Team will review the proposal and document its determination of whether: (1) the proposal meets requirements for further evaluation; (2) the State will request clarifications or corrections; or, (3) the State will determine the proposal non-responsive to the RFP and reject it.

5.2.1.2   A Proposal Evaluation Team, made up of three or more State employees, will evaluate each Technical Proposal that appears responsive to the RFP.

5.2.1.3   Each Proposal Evaluation Team member will independently, evaluate each proposal against the evaluation criteria in this RFP, rather than against other proposals, and will score each in accordance with the RFP Attachment 6.3, Technical Proposal and Evaluation Guide.

5.2.1.4   The State reserves the right, at its sole discretion, to request Proposer clarification of a Technical Proposal or to conduct clarification discussions with any or all Proposers. Any such clarification or discussion shall be limited to specific sections of the proposal identified by the State. The subject Proposer shall put any resulting clarification in writing as may be required by the State.

5.2.2   After Technical Proposal evaluations are completed, the RFP Coordinator will open the Cost Proposals and use the RFP Attachment 6.4, Cost Proposal and Scoring Guide, to calculate and document the Cost Proposal scores.

5.2.3   For each responsive proposal, the RFP Coordinator will add the average Technical Proposal score to the Cost Proposal score (refer to RFP Attachment 6.5, Proposal Score Summary Matrix).

5.3   Contract Award Process

5.3.1   The RFP Coordinator will forward the results of the proposal evaluation process to the head of the procuring agency who will consider the proposal-evaluation process results and all pertinent information available to make a determination about the contract award. The State reserves the right to make an award without further discussion of any proposal.

Notwithstanding the foregoing, to affect a contract award to a Proposer other than the one receiving the highest evaluation score, the head of the procuring agency must provide written justification for such an award and obtain the written approval of the Commissioner of Finance and Administration and the Comptroller of the Treasury.

5.3.2   After the agency head's determination, the State will issue an Evaluation Notice to identify the apparent best-evaluated proposal on the Evaluation Notice date detailed in the RFP Section 2, Schedule of Events.

NOTICE: The Evaluation Notice shall not create rights, interests, or claims of entitlement in either the Proposer with apparent best-evaluated proposal or any other Proposer.

5.3.3   The State will also make the RFP files available for public inspection on the Evaluation Notice date detailed in the RFP Section 2, Schedule of Events.

5.3.4   The Proposer with the apparent best-evaluated proposal must agree to and sign a contract with the State that shall be substantially the same as the RFP Attachment 6.1, *Pro Forma* Contract.

However, the State reserves the right, at its sole discretion, to add terms and conditions or to revise *pro forma* contract requirements in the State's best interests subsequent to this RFP process. No such terms and conditions or revision of contract requirements shall materially affect the basis of proposal evaluations or negatively impact the competitive nature of the RFP process.

5.3.5   The Proposer with the apparent best-evaluated proposal must sign and return the contract drawn by the State pursuant to this RFP no later than the Contract Signature Deadline date detailed in the RFP Section 2, Schedule of Events. If the Proposer fails to provide the signed contract by the deadline, the State may determine that the Proposer is non-responsive to the terms of this RFP and reject the proposal.

5.3.6   If the State determines that the apparent best-evaluated proposal is non-responsive and rejects the proposal after opening the Cost Proposals, the RFP Coordinator will re-calculate scores for each responsive Cost Proposal to determine the new, best–evaluated proposal.

CONTRACT
BETWEEN THE STATE GOVERNMENT,
DEPARTMENT OF FINANCE AND ADMINISTRATION
AND
CONTRACTOR NAME

This Contract, by and between the State Government, Department of Finance and Administration, hereinafter referred to as the "State" and CONTRACTOR LEGAL ENTITY NAME, hereinafter referred to as the "Contractor," is for the provision of Information Security Assessment Services as further defined in the "SCOPE OF SERVICES."

The Contractor is A/AN INDIVIDUAL, FOR-PROFIT CORPORATION, NONPROFIT CORPORATION, SPECIAL PURPOSE CORPORATION OR ASSOCIATION, PARTNERSHIP, JOINT VENTURE, OR LIMITED LIABILITY COMPANY.
Contractor Federal Employer Identification or Social Security Number: ID NUMBER
Contractor Place of Incorporation or Organization: LOCATION

A. SCOPE OF SERVICES:

A.1. The Contractor shall provide all service and deliverables as required, described, and detailed by this Scope of Services and shall meet all service and delivery timelines specified in the Scope of Services section or elsewhere in this Contract.

A.2. Statement of Work Procedures/Provisions

The purpose of this Contract is to provide a source for Information Security Assessment Services (ISAS). This Contract does not obligate the State to use the Contractor's services except as detailed in the Statement of Work Procedures/Process detailed below.

A.2.a Under the terms of this Contract and at the State's request, the Contractor will provide information security assessment services to the State using the consultants listed in Contract Section C.3, below (collectively, "consultants").

A.3 The specific roles and responsibilities of Contractor consultants shall be as defined in the Contract and future Statements of Work (SOWs).

A.4. The SOW will specify the work location(s) of Contractor consultants. Contractor consultants shall be based on-site and perform their work at State-operated, maintained, and managed facilities in Capitol City, or Contractor consultants shall be based off-site and perform their work at a Contractor location. The State reserves the right to request on-site or off-site work, whichever is deemed to be in the best interest of the project.

A.5. Standard State work schedules are based on a Monday through Friday thirty seven and one-half (37.5) hour workweek, typically comprised of five (5) seven and one-half (7.5) hour workdays, between the hours of 8:00 a.m. EST and 4:30 p.m. CST, excluding State holidays. Unless specific times are designated in the SOW, work performed under this Contract may occur during the standard State work schedule, on weekends, on State holidays, and/or at off-hours Monday through Friday. Contractor consultants will be compensated at the payment rates in Contract Section C.3., regardless of the day, date, or time the tasks are performed or the total number of hours worked during a workweek.

A.6. Contractor consultants must provide their own personal computing devices (desktop, laptop, etc.) and licenses for software installed on the devices. Commensurate with the needs of a given project, the State will provide Contractor consultants with office and meeting space, access to telephones, printers, and copiers, and connections to the Internet and/or State network. The State shall be the sole determinant with regard to facilities, supplies, access, and connections required for any given project.

A.7.   The Contractor understands and agrees that the State has executed and may execute contracts with other parties for services the same as or similar to those described herein.

A.8.   The purpose of this Contract is to establish a source of supply for information security assessment consultants. However, due to the dynamic nature of projects within State government, the State cannot predict the numbers of Contractor consultants that will be required under this Contract. Therefore, the State makes no guarantees, either stated or implied, about the demand for resources provided through this procurement. The State is not obligated to use any of the Contractor's consultants. Throughout the term of the Contract, the State retains full control and flexibility with regard to the types, quantities, and timing of Contractor consultant usage.

A.9.   Contractor Objectives and Deliverables

A.9.a. Objective 1: Provide Security Vulnerability Assessment and Penetration Testing Services

The Contractor shall conduct vulnerability assessments and penetration tests to assist in strengthening the security posture of the State Government. Vulnerability assessments and penetration testing services shall be used in identifying and validating configuration and/or technical flaws within a given system or network (i.e. firewalls, routers, servers, operating systems, applications, databases, load balancers, etc.).

A.9.b. Objective 1 Deliverables:

1. An Assessment Report outlining:

   i.   Details of the methodology used to conduct the security vulnerability assessments and penetration tests
   ii.   The results including, but not limited to, the full details of the actions taken and
   iii. The detailed documentation of security flaws and remediation recommendations of those flaws found

2. Any additional deliverables as defined in the SOW.

A.9.c. Objective 2: Provide Code Review Services

The Contractor shall conduct code review services to assist the ISAS User in strengthening the security posture of the State Government. The Contractor shall evaluate source code for programming errors that may lead to security issues (i.e. format string mistakes, buffer overflows, memory leaks, input validation/sanitization mistakes, etc.).

A.9.d. Objective 2 Deliverables:

1. A Code Review Report outlining:

   i.   Details of the methodology used to conduct code reviews
   ii.   The results including, but not limited to, the full details of the actions taken and
   iii. The detailed documentation of security flaws and remediation recommendations of those flaws found

2. Any additional deliverables as defined in the SOW.

A.9.e. Contractor must provide all software tools required to perform the tasks and deliverables as defined in the State's SOW. All costs associated with software tools must be included in the Consulting Services Hourly Rates listed in Section C.3. The State will not pay separate costs for software tools.

A.10.   Procedures/Stipulations for Providing Consultants

A.10.a. <u>Statement of Work</u>

The State will provide the Contractor with a SOW describing the requested services, including as follows:

i. Project number, which will be used to track the services through completion
ii. Description and scope of the requested services, including the specific information security and other state standard technologies involved, and any special data handling due to issues such as confidentiality
iii. Requested project timeframe and any non-standard work schedule tasks
iv. Deliverable(s)
v. Work location
vi. State Project Coordinator and
vii. Deadline for the Contractor to respond to the State's request (i.e., response period), which will be no more than five (5) business days measured from the date the SOW was distributed.

A.10.b. <u>Submission of Project Proposal.</u>

The Contractor may seek written or verbal clarifications regarding the SOW during the response period. If deemed necessary by the State, the SOW may be modified to clarify its intent and to adjust the response period accordingly.

Within the requested response period, the Contractor will respond to the SOW with a Project Proposal that includes the following:

i. Project number from the SOW
ii. Contractor understanding of the work to be performed
iii. Work plan, including a project timeframe, tasks, and resource loading
iv. Staffing plan, specifying the Consultant Classifications from Contract Section C.3 needed for the project and the hours required for each Consultant Classification
v. Maximum project consultant cost, which the Contractor shall calculate by using the payment rates per hour set forth in Section C.3.b. for each Consultant Classification needed for the project. <u>If the project timeframe spans more than one year of the Contract term, the Contractor must calculate the maximum project consultant cost using the payment rates for every effective year.</u> In other words, if the project begin and end dates lie completely within year one of the Contract term, the Contractor would calculate maximum project consultant cost using the payment rates for that Contract year. On the other hand, if the dates begin in Contract year one and extend into any portion of Contract year two, the Contractor must calculate the maximum project consultant cost using the payment rates for both years based on the dates in the Work plan. The same rule would apply for all contract years; the maximum project consultant cost must be calculated using the payment rates for the effective years. This maximum project consultant cost shall be a "not to exceed" total cost; the State shall pay no more than this cost for the consultant cost for the project, unless amended in the resulting MOU as described in Contract Section A.10.f. and
vi. Any Contractor assumptions on which the Project Proposal are based. These assumptions cannot conflict with the terms and provisions of the Contract. In the event of a conflict, the Contract will prevail.

A.10.c. The State has the sole discretion to accept the Contractor's Project Proposal, request modifications to the Contractor's Project Proposal, or to reject the Contractor's Project Proposal in its entirety.

A.10.d. <u>Project Team</u>

The Contractor shall build the gproject team for each SOW. The State reserves the right to question the composition of, and request changes to, the proposed project team.

A.10.e. <u>Memorandum of Understanding</u>

After the State has approved the Project Proposal, it will develop a Memorandum of Understanding (MOU) binding the Contractor to its Project Proposal for the associated SOW. (See Contract Attachment B for a draft of the MOU document.)

The State will provide a copy of the fully executed MOU, containing signatures from the Office for Information Resources and the Contractor, to the Contractor. Receipt of a fully executed MOU authorizes the Contractor to provide the requested services and the Contractor consultants to begin work. The State will not be liable to pay the Contractor for any work performed prior to the Contractor's receipt of a fully executed MOU.

A.10.f. Memorandum of Understanding Tracking and Amendment

The MOU will fix the maximum amount of money to be paid in compensation on a particular SOW. This amount cannot be exceeded without an MOU amendment. Such an amendment, if deemed necessary by the State, would increase the maximum potential compensation due the Contractor for the requested services. The Amendment will require the same signatures as the original MOU.

For each MOU, the Contractor will track the expenditures against the MOU Maximum Compensation, and will inform the State when expenditures are nearing either cap. If insufficient funds are remaining in the amount to complete the project, the Contractor will provide the State with a revised Project Proposal for completion of the project. The revised Project Proposal will include the same information requested in the original Project Proposal (see Contract Section A.10.b.), updated as needed to complete the project. It must also detail the reason(s) additional funds are required. The State, at its sole option, will either amend the MOU Maximum Compensation to accommodate completion of the project, in part or in whole, or direct the Contractor to cease work on the project.

A.11. Contractor Consultant Performance and Replacement

A.11.a. The State shall be the sole judge of the quality of services provided and the project progress achieved by the Contractor's consultants. The Contractor agrees to remove and replace at the Contractor's expense, consultants whom the State judges to be incompetent, careless, unsuitable or otherwise objectionable, or whose continued use is deemed contrary to the best interests of the State or deemed not to make substantial contributions to the project. The Contractor agrees not to charge the State for services performed which the State designates as being unacceptable.

This provision will not be deemed to give the State the right to require the Contractor to terminate any Contractor employee's employment. Rather, this provision is intended to give the State only the right to require that the Contractor discontinue using an employee in the performance of services for the State.

A.11.b. At the State's request, the Contractor will replace an individual who has voluntarily withdrawn or that the Contractor has voluntarily removed from State assignment. Any requirement for such replacement will be at the State's sole discretion; the State is not obligated to accept replacement of removed or withdrawn consultants. The State will compensate the Contractor for acceptable services completed by the consultant prior to voluntary withdrawal or removal.

A.11.c. If the State requests a replacement as described in Contract Sections A.11.a. and A.11.b., the Contractor will replace the consultant with a consultant of equal or greater years experience as the consultant proposed in the associated Project Proposal for the MOU. The Contractor will be compensated for the replacement consultant at the rate established for the original consultant.

A.11.d. The termination of an individual consultant's assignment will not necessarily result in the termination of the MOU related to that consultant.

A.12. Miscellaneous Policies and Procedures

A.12.a. The State will <u>not</u> provide parking for Contractor consultants.

A.12.b. Contractor consultants do <u>not</u> have access to the State clinic.

A.13. <u>Information Security Compliance</u>

Contractor warrants to the State that it will cooperate with the State in the course of performance of the Contract so that both parties will be in compliance with State Government's Enterprise Security Policies requirements and any other state and federal computer security regulations including cooperation and coordination with the State's Office for Information Resources Security Management Team and other compliance officers required by its regulations. The Enterprise Security Policies can be found on the State's public website at:

http://www.state.tn.us/finance/oir/security/secpolicy.html

A.14. <u>State's Technical Architecture</u>

Contractor consultants shall provide all services requested through this Contract within the context of the technical environment described by the State Information Resources Architecture.

A.15. <u>Periodic Meetings</u>

The State reserves the right, at the State's option, to request periodic meetings with Contractor management staff to discuss topics including, but not limited to, the following: general project direction, management, and coordination; State technical infrastructure and standards; SOW Clarifications; and time keeping and other project progress records. At the State's sole discretion, these meetings shall occur at a State location or via conference call and shall be at no additional cost to the State.

A.16. <u>Provision of Managed Security Services Disallowed</u>

The Contractor shall not have active managed-security service provider contract(s) with, or otherwise provide managed security services to, any other State Government agency during the term of this Contract.

B. CONTRACT TERM:

This Contract shall be effective for the period commencing on July 2, 2008 and ending on July 1, 2011. The State shall have no obligation for services rendered by the Contractor that are not performed within the specified period.

C. PAYMENT TERMS AND CONDITIONS:

C.1. <u>Maximum Liability</u>. In no event shall the maximum liability of the State under this Contract exceed WRITTEN DOLLAR AMOUNT ($NUMBER). The payment rates in Section C.3 shall constitute the entire compensation due the Contractor for the Service and all of the Contractor's obligations hereunder regardless of the difficulty, materials, or equipment required. The payment rates include, but are not limited to, all applicable taxes, fees, overheads, and all other direct and indirect costs incurred or to be incurred by the Contractor.

The Contractor is not entitled to be paid the maximum liability for any period under the Contract or any extensions of the Contract for work not requested by the State. The maximum liability represents available funds for payment to the Contractor and does not guarantee payment of any such funds to the Contractor under this Contract unless the State requests work and the Contractor performs said work. In which case, the Contractor shall be paid in accordance with the payment rates detailed in Section C.3. The State is under no obligation to request work from the Contractor in any specific dollar amounts or to request any work at all from the Contractor during any period of this Contract.

C.2. <u>Compensation Firm</u>. The payment rates and the maximum liability of the State under this Contract are firm for the duration of the Contract and are not subject to escalation for any reason unless amended.

C.3. <u>Payment Methodology</u>. The Contractor shall be compensated based on the payment rates herein for units of service authorized by the State in a total amount not to exceed the Contract Maximum Liability established in Section C.1.

    a. The Contractor's compensation shall be contingent upon the satisfactory completion of units, milestones, or increments of service defined in Section A.

    b. The Contractor shall be compensated for said units, milestones, or increments of service based upon the following payment rates:

Consulting Services Hourly Rates			
Consultant Classifications	**Year 07/02/11-07/01/12**	**Year 07/02/12-07/01/13**	**Year 07/02/13-07/01/14**
Consultant With Greater Than 15 Years Information Security-Related Experience	$[HOURLY RATE]	$[HOURLY RATE]	$[HOURLY RATE]
Consultant With 10 Years To 15 Years Information Security-Related Experience	$[HOURLY RATE]	$[HOURLY RATE]	$[HOURLY RATE]
Consultant With 5 Years To Less Than 10 Years Information Security-Related Experience	$[HOURLY RATE]	$[HOURLY RATE]	$[HOURLY RATE]
Consultant With Less Than 5 Years Information Security-Related Experience	$[HOURLY RATE]	$[HOURLY RATE]	$[HOURLY RATE]

    c. The Contractor shall not be compensated for travel time to the primary location of service provision.

    d. The Contractor hourly payment rates shall be fully loaded to include all administrative, software tool, and travel costs. The State will not pay any costs for projects apart from hourly payment rates.

C.4. <u>Travel Compensation</u>. The Contractor shall not be compensated or reimbursed for travel, meals, or lodging.

C.5. <u>Invoice Requirements</u>. The Contractor shall invoice the State only for completed increments of service and for the amount stipulated in Section C.3, above, and as required below prior to any payment.

    a. The Contractor shall submit invoices no more often than monthly, with all necessary supporting documentation, to

        John Doe, Chief Information Security Officer
        Department of Finance and Administration, Office of Information Resources
        State Government Tower

100 1st Avenue
Capitol City, NY 12345-1200
Ph: 866-555-1212
Fax: 866-555-1213

b. The Contractor agrees that each invoice submitted shall clearly and accurately (all calculations must be extended and totaled correctly) detail the following required information:

(1) Invoice/Reference Number (assigned by the Contractor)
(2) Invoice Date
(3) Invoice Period (period to which all invoiced charges are applicable)
(4) Contract Number (assigned by the State to this Contract)
(5) Account Name: Department of Finance and Administration, Division of Security Policy & Audit
(6) Account/Customer Number (uniquely assigned by the Contractor to the above-referenced Account Name)
(7) Contractor Name
(8) Contractor Federal Employer Identification Number or Social Security Number (as referenced in this Contract)
(9) Contractor Contact (name, phone, and/or fax for the individual to contact with billing questions)
(10) Contractor Remittance Address
(11) Complete Itemization of Charges, which shall detail the following:

i. Service or Milestone Description including name/title and MOU Project Number of each service invoiced
ii. Number of Completed Units, Increments, Hours, or Days as applicable, of each service invoiced
iii. Applicable Payment Rate (as stipulated in Section C.3.) of each service invoiced
iv. Amount Due by Service and
v. Total Amount Due for the invoice period

c. The Contractor understands and agrees that an invoice to the State under this Contract shall:

(1) include only charges for service described in Contract Section A and in accordance with payment terms and conditions set forth in Contract Section C;
(2) not include any future work but will only be submitted for completed service and
(3) not include sales tax or shipping charges

d. The Contractor agrees that timeframe for payment (and any discounts) begins when the State is in receipt of each invoice meeting the minimum requirements above.

e. The Contractor shall complete and sign a "Substitute W-9 Form" provided to the Contractor by the State. The taxpayer identification number contained in the Substitute W-9 submitted to the State shall agree with the Federal Employer Identification Number or Social Security Number referenced in this Contract for the Contractor. The Contractor shall not invoice the State for services until the State has received this completed form.

C.6. Payment of Invoice. The payment of the Invoice by the State shall not prejudice the State's right to object to or question any invoice or matter in relation thereto. Such payment by the State shall neither be construed as acceptance of any part of the work or service provided nor as an approval of any of the amounts invoiced therein.

C.7.   <u>Invoice Reductions</u>. The Contractor's Invoice shall be subject to reduction for amounts included in any invoice or payment theretofore made which are determined by the State, on the basis of audits conducted in accordance with the terms of this Contract, not to constitute proper remuneration for compensable services.

C.8.   <u>Deductions</u>. The State reserves the right to deduct from amounts which are or shall become due and payable to the Contractor—under this or any Contract between the Contractor and the State Government—any amounts which are or shall become due and payable to the State Government by the Contractor.

C.9.   <u>Automatic Deposits</u>. The Contractor shall complete and sign an "Authorization Agreement for Automatic Deposit (ACH Credits) Form." This form shall be provided to the Contractor by the State. Once this form has been completed and submitted to the State by the Contractor all payments to the Contractor, under this or any other Contract the Contractor has with the State Government shall be made by Automated Clearing House (ACH). The Contractor shall not invoice the State for services until the Contractor has completed this form and submitted it to the State.

D.   STANDARD TERMS AND CONDITIONS:

D.1.   <u>Required Approvals</u>. The State is not bound by this Contract until it is approved by the appropriate State officials in accordance with applicable State laws and regulations.

D.2.   <u>Modification and Amendment</u>. This Contract may be modified only by a written amendment executed by all parties hereto and approved by the appropriate State officials in accordance with applicable State laws and regulations.

D.3.   <u>Termination for Convenience</u>. The State may terminate this Contract without cause for any reason. Said termination shall not be deemed a Breach of Contract by the State. The State shall give the Contractor at least thirty (30) days written notice before the effective termination date. The Contractor shall be entitled to receive compensation for satisfactory, authorized service completed as of the termination date, but in no event shall the State be liable to the Contractor for compensation for any service which has not been rendered. Upon such termination, the Contractor shall have no right to any actual general, special, incidental, consequential, or any other damages whatsoever of any description or amount.

D.4.   <u>Termination for Cause</u>. If the Contractor fails to properly perform the obligations under this Contract in a timely or proper manner, or if the Contractor violates any terms of this Contract, the State shall have the right to immediately terminate the Contract and withhold payments in excess of fair compensation for completed services. Notwithstanding the above, the Contractor shall not be relieved of liability to the State for damages sustained by virtue of any breach of this Contract by the Contractor.

D.5.   <u>Subcontracting</u>. The Contractor shall not assign this Contract or enter into a subcontract for any of the services performed under this Contract without obtaining the prior written approval of the State. If such subcontracts are approved by the State, they shall contain, at a minimum, sections of this Contract below pertaining to "Conflicts of Interest," "Nondiscrimination," and "Records" (as identified by the section headings). Notwithstanding any use of approved subcontractors, the Contractor shall be the prime contractor and shall be responsible for all work performed.

D.6.   <u>Conflicts of Interest</u>. The Contractor warrants that no part of the total Contract Amount shall be paid directly or indirectly to an employee or official of the State Government as wages, compensation, or gifts in exchange for acting as an officer, agent, employee, subcontractor, or consultant to the Contractor in connection with any work contemplated or performed relative to this Contract.

D.7. <u>Nondiscrimination</u>. The Contractor hereby agrees, warrants, and assures that no person shall be excluded from participation in, be denied benefits of, or be otherwise subjected to discrimination in the performance of this Contract or in the employment practices of the Contractor on the grounds of disability, age, race, color, religion, sex, national origin, or any other classification protected by federal, state, constitutional, or statutory law. The Contractor shall, upon request, show proof of such nondiscrimination and shall post in conspicuous places, available to all employees and applicants, notices of nondiscrimination.

D.8. <u>Prohibition of Illegal Immigrants</u>. The requirements of Public Acts of 2006, Chapter Number 878, of the State Government, addressing the use of illegal immigrants in the performance of any Contract to supply goods or services to the State Government, shall be a material provision of this Contract, a breach of which shall be grounds for monetary and other penalties, up to and including termination of this Contract.

    a. The Contractor hereby attests, certifies, warrants, and assures that the Contractor shall not knowingly utilize the services of an illegal immigrant in the performance of this Contract and shall not knowingly utilize the services of any subcontractor who will utilize the services of an illegal immigrant in the performance of this Contract. The Contractor shall reaffirm this attestation, in writing, by submitting to the State a completed and signed copy of the document at Attachment A, hereto, semiannually during the period of this Contract. Such attestations shall be maintained by the Contractor and made available to state officials upon request.

    b. Prior to the use of any subcontractor in the performance of this Contract, and semiannually thereafter, during the period of this Contract, the Contractor shall obtain and retain a current, written attestation that the subcontractor shall not knowingly utilize the services of an illegal immigrant to perform work relative to this Contract and shall not knowingly utilize the services of any subcontractor who will utilize the services of an illegal immigrant to perform work relative to this Contract. Attestations obtained from such subcontractors shall be maintained by the Contractor and made available to state officials upon request.

    c. The Contractor shall maintain records for all personnel used in the performance of this Contract. Said records shall be subject to review and random inspection at any reasonable time upon reasonable notice by the State.

    d. The Contractor understands and agrees that failure to comply with this section will be subject to the sanctions of Public Chapter 878 of 2006 for acts or omissions occurring after its effective date. This law requires the Commissioner of Finance and Administration to prohibit a contractor from contracting with, or submitting an offer, proposal, or bid to contract with the State Government to supply goods or services for a period of one year after a contractor is discovered to have knowingly used the services of illegal immigrants during the performance of this Contract.

    e. For purposes of this Contract, "illegal immigrant" shall be defined as any person who is not either a United States citizen, a Lawful Permanent Resident, or a person whose physical presence in the United States is authorized or allowed by the federal Department of Homeland Security and who, under federal immigration laws and/or regulations, is authorized to be employed in the U.S. or is otherwise authorized to provide services under the Contract.

D.9. <u>Records</u>. The Contractor shall maintain documentation for all charges under this Contract. The books, records, and documents of the Contractor, insofar as they relate to work performed or money received under this Contract, shall be maintained for a period of three (3) full years from the date of the final payment and shall be subject to audit at any reasonable time and upon reasonable notice by the State, the Comptroller of the Treasury, or their duly appointed representatives. The financial statements shall be prepared in accordance with generally accepted accounting principles.

D.10. Monitoring. The Contractor's activities conducted and records maintained pursuant to this Contract shall be subject to monitoring and evaluation by the State, the Comptroller of the Treasury, or their duly appointed representatives.

D.11. Progress Reports. The Contractor shall submit brief, periodic, progress reports to the State as requested.

D.12. Strict Performance. Failure by any party to this Contract to insist in any one or more cases upon the strict performance of any of the terms, covenants, conditions, or provisions of this Contract shall not be construed as a waiver or relinquishment of any such term, covenant, condition, or provision. No term or condition of this Contract shall be held to be waived, modified, or deleted except by a written amendment signed by the parties hereto.

D.13. Independent Contractor. The parties hereto, in the performance of this Contract, shall not act as employees, partners, joint venturers, or associates of one another. It is expressly acknowledged by the parties hereto that such parties are independent contracting entities and that nothing in this Contract shall be construed to create an employer/employee relationship or to allow either to exercise control or direction over the manner or method by which the other transacts its business affairs or provides its usual services. The employees or agents of one party shall not be deemed or construed to be the employees or agents of the other party for any purpose whatsoever.

The Contractor, being an independent contractor and not an employee of the State, agrees to carry adequate public liability and other appropriate forms of insurance, including adequate public liability and other appropriate forms of insurance on the Contractor's employees, and to pay all applicable taxes incident to this Contract.

D.14. State Liability. The State shall have no liability except as specifically provided in this Contract.

D.15. *Force Majeure*. The obligations of the parties to this Contract are subject to prevention by causes beyond the parties' control that could not be avoided by the exercise of due care including, but not limited to, acts of God, natural disasters, riots, wars, epidemics, or any other similar cause.

D.16. State and Federal Compliance. The Contractor shall comply with all applicable State and Federal laws and regulations in the performance of this Contract.

D.17. Governing Law. This Contract shall be governed by and construed in accordance with the laws of the State Government. The Contractor agrees that it will be subject to the exclusive jurisdiction of the courts of the State Government in actions that may arise under this Contract. The Contractor acknowledges and agrees that any rights or claims against the State Government or its employees hereunder, and any remedies arising therefrom, shall be subject to and limited to those rights and remedies, if any, available under *State Code Annotated*, Sections 9-8-101 through 9-8-407.

D.18. Completeness. This Contract is complete and contains the entire understanding between the parties relating to the subject matter contained herein, including all the terms and conditions of the parties' agreement. This Contract supersedes any and all prior understandings, representations, negotiations, and agreements between the parties relating hereto, whether written or oral.

D.19. Severability. If any terms and conditions of this Contract are held to be invalid or unenforceable as a matter of law, the other terms and conditions hereof shall not be affected thereby and shall remain in full force and effect. To this end, the terms and conditions of this Contract are declared severable.

D.20. Headings. Section headings of this Contract are for reference purposes only and shall not be construed as part of this Contract.

E. SPECIAL TERMS AND CONDITIONS:

E.1. Conflicting Terms and Conditions. Should any of these special terms and conditions conflict with any other terms and conditions of this Contract, these special terms and conditions shall control.

E.2. Communications and Contacts. All instructions, notices, consents, demands, or other communications required or contemplated by this Contract shall be in writing and shall be made by certified, first class mail, return receipt requested and postage prepaid, by overnight courier service with an asset-tracking system, or by EMAIL or facsimile transmission with recipient confirmation. Any such communications, regardless of method of transmission, shall be addressed to the respective party at the appropriate mailing address, facsimile number, or EMAIL address as set forth below or to that of such other party or address, as may be hereafter specified by written notice.

The State:

John Doe, Chief Information Security Officer
Department of Finance and Administration
State Government Tower
100 1st Avenue
Capitol City, NY 12345-1200
John.Doe@state.ny.us
Ph: 866-555-1212
Fax: 866-555-1213

The Contractor:

NAME & TITLE OF CONTRACTOR CONTACT PERSON
CONTRACTOR NAME
ADDRESS
EMAIL ADDRESS
Telephone # NUMBER
FAX # NUMBER

All instructions, notices, consents, demands, or other communications shall be considered effectively given upon receipt or recipient confirmation as may be required.

E.3. Subject to Funds Availability. The Contract is subject to the appropriation and availability of State and/or Federal funds. In the event that the funds are not appropriated or are otherwise unavailable, the State reserves the right to terminate the Contract upon written notice to the Contractor. Said termination shall not be deemed a breach of Contract by the State. Upon receipt of the written notice, the Contractor shall cease all work associated with the Contract. Should such an event occur, the Contractor shall be entitled to compensation for all satisfactory and authorized services completed as of the termination date. Upon such termination, the Contractor shall have no right to recover from the State any actual, general, special, incidental, consequential, or any other damages whatsoever of any description or amount.

E.4. State Consolidated Retirement System. The Contractor acknowledges and understands that, subject to statutory exceptions contained in *State Code Annotated*, Section 8-36-801, *et. seq.*, the law governing the State Consolidated Retirement System (TCRS), provides that if a retired member of TCRS, or of any superseded system administered by TCRS, or of any local retirement fund established pursuant to *State Code Annotated*, Title 8, Chapter 35, Part 3 accepts state employment, the member's retirement allowance is suspended during the period of the employment. Accordingly and notwithstanding any provision of this Contract to the contrary, the Contractor agrees that if it is later determined that the true nature of the working relationship between the Contractor and the State under this Contract is that of "employee/employer" and not that of an independent contractor, the Contractor may be required to repay to TCRS the amount of retirement benefits the Contractor received from TCRS during the period of this Contract.

E.5.   Incorporation of Additional Documents. Included in this Contract by reference are the following documents:

a.   The Contract document and its attachments

b.   The Memoranda of Understandings (MOU), their associated addenda, Statements of Work (SOWs), and Project Proposals

c.   All Clarifications and addenda made to the Contractor's Proposal

d.   The Request for Proposal and its associated amendments

e.   Technical Specifications provided to the Contractor

f.   The Contractor's Proposal

In the event of a discrepancy or ambiguity regarding the Contractor's duties, responsibilities, and performance under this Contract, these documents shall govern in order of precedence detailed above.

E.6.   Contractor Commitment to Diversity. The Contractor shall comply with and make reasonable business efforts to exceed the commitment to diversity represented by the Contractor's proposal responding to RFP-317.03-181-08 (Attachment 6.3, Section B, Item B.13.) and resulting in this Contract.

The Contractor shall assist the State in monitoring the Contractor's performance of this commitment by providing, as requested, a quarterly report of participation in the performance of this Contract by small business enterprises and businesses owned by minorities, women, and persons with a disability. Such reports shall be provided to the State Government Governor's Office of Business Diversity Enterprise in form and substance as required by said office.

E.7.   State Ownership of Work Products. The State shall have ownership, right, title, and interest, including ownership of copyright, in all work products, including computer source code, created, designed, developed, derived, documented, installed, or delivered under this Contract subject to the next subsection and full and final payment for each "Work Product." The State shall have royalty-free and unlimited rights and license to use, disclose, reproduce, publish, distribute, modify, maintain, or create derivative works from, for any purpose whatsoever, all said Work Products.

a.   To the extent that the Contractor uses any of its preexisting, proprietary, or independently developed tools, materials, or information ("Contractor Materials"), the Contractor shall retain all right, title, and interest in and to such Contractor Materials, and the State shall acquire no right, title, or interest in or to such Contractor Materials EXCEPT the Contractor grants to the State an unlimited, non-transferable license to use, copy, and distribute internally, solely for the State's internal purposes, any Contractor Materials reasonably associated with any Work Product provided under the Contract.

b.   The Contractor shall furnish such information and data as the State may request, including but not limited to computer code, that is applicable, essential, fundamental, or intrinsic to any Work Product and Contractor Materials reasonably associated with any Work Product, in accordance with this Contract and applicable state law.

c.   Nothing in this Contract shall prohibit the Contractor's use for its own purposes of the general knowledge, skills, experience, ideas, concepts, know-how, and techniques obtained and used during the course of providing the services requested under this Contract.

d. Nothing in the Contract shall prohibit the Contractor from developing for itself, or for others, materials that are similar to and/or competitive with those that are produced under this Contract.

E.8. State Furnished Property. The Contractor shall be responsible for the correct use, maintenance, and protection of all articles of nonexpendable, tangible, personal property furnished by the State for the Contractor's temporary use under this Contract. Upon termination of this Contract, all property furnished shall be returned to the State in good order and condition as when received, reasonable use and wear thereof excepted. Should the property be destroyed, lost, or stolen, the Contractor shall be responsible to the State for the residual value of the property at the time of loss.

E.9. Prohibited Advertising. The Contractor shall not refer to this Contract or the Contractor's relationship with the State hereunder in commercial advertising in such a manner as to state or imply that the Contractor or the Contractor's services are endorsed. It is expressly understood and agreed that the obligations set forth in this section shall survive the termination of this Contract in perpetuity.

E.10. Debarment and Suspension. The Contractor certifies, to the best of its knowledge and belief, that it, its current and future principals, its current and future subcontractors and their principals:

a. are not presently debarred, suspended, proposed for debarment, declared ineligible, or voluntarily excluded from covered transactions by any federal or state department or agency

b. have not been convicted of, or had a civil judgment rendered against them from commission of fraud, or a criminal offence in connection with obtaining, attempting to obtain, or performing a public (federal, state, or local) transaction or grant under a public transaction; violation of federal or state antitrust statutes or commission of embezzlement, theft, forgery, bribery, falsification, or destruction of records, making false statements, or receiving stolen property

c. are not presently indicted or otherwise criminally or civilly charged by a government entity (federal, state, or local) with commission of any of the offenses detailed in section b. of this certification and

d. have not within a three (3) year period preceding this Contract had one or more public transactions (federal, state, or local) terminated for cause or default.

The Contractor shall provide immediate written notice to the State if at any time it learns that there was an earlier failure to disclose information or that due to changed circumstances, its principals or the principals of its subcontractors are excluded or disqualified.

E.11. Limitation of Liability. The parties agree that the total liability of the Contractor for breach of this Contract shall not exceed two (2) times the value of this Contract. The value shall be established by the Contract Maximum Liability in Section C.1 and increased by subsequent amendments if any. The foregoing provision shall not limit the Contractor's liability for intentional torts, criminal acts, or fraudulent conduct.

E.13. HIPAA Compliance. The State and Contractor shall comply with obligations under the Health Insurance Portability and Accountability Act of 1996 (HIPAA) and its accompanying regulations.

a.	Contractor warrants to the State that it is familiar with the requirements of HIPAA and its accompanying regulations, and will comply with all applicable HIPAA requirements in the course of this Contract.

b.	Contractor warrants that it will cooperate with the State, including cooperation and coordination with State privacy officials and other compliance officers required by HIPAA and its regulations, in the course of performance of the Contract so that both parties will be in compliance with HIPAA.

c.	The State and the Contractor will sign documents, including but not limited to business associate agreements (see Contract Attachment C), as required by HIPAA and that are reasonably necessary to keep the State and Contractor in compliance with HIPAA. This provision shall not apply if information received by the State under this Contract is NOT "protected health information" as defined by HIPAA, or if HIPAA permits the State to receive such information without entering into a business associate agreement or signing another such document.

E.14.	Confidentiality of Records. All information relating to State information technology systems is confidential information and shall not be disclosed without written consent of the Chief Information Officer, Department of Finance and Administration. This confidentiality obligation applies to all forms of communication including written reports, notes, and verbal communications, and applies regardless of whether the same or similar information has been divulged by the State or other persons.

Contractor shall restrict access to confidential information to those individuals within the Contractor's organization who need such access in order to provide the information security assessment services to the State. Prior to such access, Contractor shall advise each such individual of the confidential nature of the records and information and each such individual shall agree to be bound by the terms hereof.

Any disclosure or loss of State confidential information shall immediately be reported to the Chief Information Officer. Contractor will fully cooperate with the State and its authorized agents in any investigation of the disclosure or loss of State confidential information.

The Contractor will indemnify the State and hold it harmless for any claims, fines, litigation, and any other expenses caused by the contractor's disclosure or loss of State confidential information. No limitation of the contractor's liability will apply to this obligation, regardless of any other provisions of this contract limiting the liability of the contractor for damages.

It is expressly understood and agreed the obligations set forth in this section shall survive the termination of this Contract.

E.15.	Partial Takeover. The State may, at its convenience and without cause, exercise a partial takeover of any service which the Contractor is obligated to perform under this Contract, including but not limited to any service which is the subject of a subcontract between Contractor and a third party, although the Contractor is not in Breach (hereinafter referred to as "Partial Takeover"). Said Partial Takeover shall not be deemed a Breach of Contract by the State. Contractor shall be given at least 30 days prior written notice of said Partial Takeover with said notice to specify the area(s) of service the State will assume and the date of said assumption. Any Partial Takeover by the State shall not alter in any way Contractor's other obligations under this Contract. The State may withhold from amounts due the Contractor the amount the Contractor would have been paid to deliver the service as determined by the State. The amounts shall be withheld effective as of the date the State assumes the service. Upon Partial Takeover, the Contractor shall have no right to recover from the State any actual, general, special, incidental, consequential, or any other damages whatsoever of any description or amount.

E.16. <u>Unencumbered Personnel</u>. All persons assigned by the Contractor to perform services for the State under this Contract, whether they are employees, agents, subcontractors, or principals of the Contractor, shall not be subject to any employment contract or restrictive covenant provisions that would preclude those persons for performing the same or similar services for the State after the termination of this Contract, either as a State employee, an independent contractor, or an employee, agent, subcontractor, or principal of another contractor with the State. If the Contractor provides the State with the services of any person subject to a restrictive covenant or contractual provision in violation of this provision, any such restrictive covenant or contractual provision will be void and unenforceable, and the Contractor will pay the State and any person involved all of its expenses, including attorneys fees, caused by attempts to enforce such provisions.

E.17. <u>Insurance</u>. The Contractor shall carry adequate liability and other appropriate forms of insurance.

    a.   The Contractor shall maintain, at minimum, the following insurance coverage:

        (1)   Workers' Compensation/Employers' Liability (including all states coverage) with a limit not less than the relevant statutory amount or one million dollars ($1,000,000) per occurrence for employers' liability whichever is greater.

        (2)   Comprehensive Commercial General Liability (including personal injury & property damage, premises/operations, independent contractor, contractual liability, and completed operations/products) with a bodily injury/property damage combined single limit not less than one million dollars ($1,000,000) per occurrence and two million dollars ($2,000,000) aggregate.

    b.   At any time State may require the Contractor to provide a valid Certificate of Insurance detailing Coverage Description; Insurance Company & Policy Number; Exceptions and Exclusions; Policy Effective Date; Policy Expiration Date; Limit(s) of Liability; and Name and Address of Insured. Failure to provide required evidence of insurance coverage shall be a material breach of this Contract.

IN WITNESS WHEREOF:

CONTRACTOR LEGAL ENTITY NAME:

_____

CONTRACTOR SIGNATURE   **DATE**

_____

PRINTED NAME AND TITLE OF CONTRACTOR SIGNATORY (above)

DEPARTMENT OF FINANCE AND ADMINISTRATION:

_____

COMMISSIONER   **DATE**

APPROVED:

_____

COMMISSIONER   **DATE**
DEPARTMENT OF FINANCE AND ADMINISTRATION

_____

COMPTROLLER OF THE TREASURY   **DATE**

ATTESTATION RE PERSONNEL USED IN CONTRACT PERFORMANCE

SUBJECT CONTRACT NUMBER:	
CONTRACTOR LEGAL ENTITY NAME:	
FEDERAL EMPLOYER IDENTIFICATION NUMBER: (or Social Security Number)	

The Contractor, identified above, does hereby attest, certify, warrant, and assure that the Contractor shall not knowingly utilize the services of an illegal immigrant in the performance of this Contract and shall not knowingly utilize the services of any subcontractor who will utilize the services of an illegal immigrant in the performance of this Contract.

CONTRACTOR SIGNATURE

NOTICE: This attestation MUST be signed by an individual empowered to contractually bind the Contractor. If said individual is not the chief executive or president, this document shall attach evidence showing the individual's authority to contractually bind the Contractor.

PRINTED NAME AND TITLE OF SIGNATORY

DATE OF ATTESTATION

MEMORANDUM OF UNDERSTANDING
BETWEEN THE
STATE GOVERNMENT
Department of Finance and Administration
and

CONTRACTOR LEGAL ENTITY NAME
for
Project

This agreement, by and between the State Government, Department of **Finance & Administration, Office for Information Resources**, hereinafter referred to as the "State" and **CONTRACTOR LEGAL ENTITY NAME**, hereinafter referred to as the "Contractor" is as follows:

The Contractor understands and agrees that this Memorandum of Understanding (MOU) is governed by the provisions of Department of Finance and Administration Contract Number **FA-##-#####-##**, hereinafter referred to as the "Master Contract." In the provision of services pursuant to this MOU, the Contractor will conform to these provisions in their entirety.

The Contractor will provide the services as described in this MOU and its addenda, Statement of Work and Project Proposal, which are attached hereto. In the event of a conflict between the MOU (and its addenda) and the Master Contract, the documents shall govern in the order of preference given in the Master Contract.

This MOU shall be effective for the period commencing on DATE and ending on DATE, unless amended.

In no event shall the maximum liability of the State under this MOU exceed $AMOUNT, unless amended. For the services provided pursuant to this MOU, the maximum liability amount shall constitute the entire potential compensation due the Contractor for the services and all of the Contractor's obligations hereunder regardless of the difficulty, or materials or equipment required.

The Contractor shall be compensated and invoices submitted in accordance with the provisions of the Master Contract.

The State may, at any time and for any reason, terminate this MOU in accordance with the provisions of the Master Contract.

This agreement may be modified only by a written amendment that has been executed and approved by the appropriate State officials as indicated below:

_____

MOU Signatures:

CONTRACTOR LEGAL ENTITY NAME

_____

NAME AND TITLE OF CONTRACTOR SIGNATORY　　　　　　　**DATE**

DEPARTMENT OF FINANCE AND ADMINISTRATION, OFFICE FOR INFORMATION RESOURCES

_____

NAME AND TITLE OF STATE PROJECT COORDINATOR   DATE

_____

John Doe, CISO   DATE

HIPAA BUSINESS ASSOCIATE AGREEMENT
COMPLIANCE WITH PRIVACY AND SECURITY RULES

THIS BUSINESS ASSOCIATE AGREEMENT (hereinafter "Agreement") is between The State Government, Department of Finance and Administration (hereinafter "Covered Entity") and _____ (hereinafter "Business Associate"). Covered Entity and Business Associate may be referred to herein individually as "Party" or collectively as "Parties."

BACKGROUND

Covered Entity acknowledges that it is subject to the Privacy and Security Rules (45 CFR Parts 160 and 164) promulgated by the United States Department of Health and Human Services pursuant to the Health Insurance Portability and Accountability Act of 1996 (HIPAA), Public Law 104-191 in certain aspects of its operations.

Business Associate provides services to Covered Entity pursuant to one or more contractual relationships detailed below and hereinafter referred to as "Service Contracts"

Contract Awarded Pursuant to RFP # 427.04-107-08

In the course of executing Service Contracts, Business Associate may come into contact with, use, or disclose Protected Health Information (defined in Section 1.8 below). Said Service Contracts are hereby incorporated by reference and shall be taken and considered as a part of this document the same as if fully set out herein.

In accordance with the federal privacy and security regulations set forth at 45 C.F.R. Part 160 and Part 164, Subparts A, C, and E, which require Covered Entity to have a written memorandum with each of its internal Business Associates, the Parties wish to establish satisfactory assurances that Business Associate will appropriately safeguard "Protected Health Information" and, therefore, make this Agreement.

DEFINITIONS

1.1 Terms used, but not otherwise defined, in this Agreement shall have the same meaning as those terms in 45 CFR §§ 160.103, 164.103, 164.304, 164.501 and 164.504.

1.2 "Designated Record Set" shall have the meaning set out in its definition at 45 C.F.R. § 164.501.

1.3 "Electronic Protected Health Care Information" shall have the meaning set out in its definition at 45 C.F.R. § 160.103.

1.4 "Health Care Operations" shall have the meaning set out in its definition at 45 C.F.R. § 164.501.

1.5 "Individual" shall have the same meaning as the term "individual" in 45 CFR § 160.103 and shall include a person who qualifies as a personal representative in accordance with 45 CFR § 164.502(g).

1.6 "Privacy Official" shall have the meaning as set out in its definition at 45 C.F.R. § 164.530(a)(1).

1.7 "Privacy Rule" shall mean the Standards for Privacy of Individually Identifiable Health Information at 45 CFR Part 160 and Part 164, subparts A, and E.

1.8 "Protected Health Information" shall have the same meaning as the term "protected health information" in 45 CFR § 160.103, limited to the information created or received by Business Associate from or on behalf of Covered Entity.

1.9 "Required by Law" shall have the meaning set forth in 45 CFR § 164.512.

1.10 "Security Rule" shall mean the Security Standards for the Protection of Electronic Protected

Health Information at 45 CFR Parts 160 and 164, Subparts A and C.

2. OBLIGATIONS AND ACTIVITIES OF BUSINESS ASSOCIATE (Privacy Rule)

2.1 Business Associate agrees to fully comply with the requirements under the Privacy Rule applicable to "business associates," as that term is defined in the Privacy Rule and not use or further disclose Protected Health Information other than as permitted or required by this Agreement, the Service Contracts, or as Required by Law. In case of any conflict between this Agreement and the Service Contracts, this Agreement shall govern.

2.2 Business Associate agrees to use appropriate procedural, physical, and electronic safeguards to prevent use or disclosure of Protected Health Information other than as provided for by this Agreement. Said safeguards shall include, but are not limited to, requiring employees to agree to use or disclose Protected Health Information only as permitted or required by this Agreement and taking related disciplinary actions for inappropriate use or disclosure as necessary.

2.3 Business Associate shall require any agent, including a subcontractor, to whom it provides Protected Health Information received from, created, or received by, Business Associate on behalf of Covered Entity or that carries out any duties for the Business Associate involving the use, custody, disclosure, creation of, or access to Protected Health Information, to agree, by written contract with Business Associate, to the same restrictions and conditions that apply through this Agreement to Business Associate with respect to such information.

2.4 Business Associate agrees to mitigate, to the extent practicable, any harmful effect that is known to Business Associate of a use or disclosure of Protected Health Information by Business Associate in violation of the requirements of this Agreement.

2.5 Business Associate agrees to require its employees, agents, and subcontractors to promptly report, to Business Associate, any use or disclosure of Protected Health Information in violation of this Agreement. Business Associate agrees to report to Covered Entity any use or disclosure of the Protected Health Information not provided for by this Agreement.

2.6 If Business Associate receives Protected Health Information from Covered Entity in a Designated Record Set, then Business Associate agrees to provide access, at the request of Covered Entity, to Protected Health Information in a Designated Record Set, to Covered Entity or, as directed by covered Entity, to an Individual in order to meet the requirements under 45 CFR § 164.524, provided that Business Associate shall have at least twenty (20) business days from Covered Entity notice to provide access to or deliver such information.

2.7 If Business Associate receives Protected Health Information from Covered Entity in a Designated Record Set, then Business Associate agrees to make any amendments to Protected Health Information in a Designated Record Set that the Covered Entity directs or agrees to pursuant to the 45 CFR § 164.526 at the request of Covered Entity or an Individual, and in the time and manner designated by Covered Entity, provided that Business Associate shall have at least ten (10) days from Covered Entity notice to make an amendment.

2.8 Business Associate agrees to make its internal practices, books, and records including policies and procedures and Protected Health Information, relating to the use and disclosure of Protected Health Information received from, created by, or received by Business Associate on behalf of, Covered Entity available to the Secretary of the United States Department of Health and Human Services or the Secretary's designee, in a time and manner designated by the Secretary, for purposes of determining Covered Entity's or Business Associate's compliance with the Privacy Rule.

2.9 Business Associate agrees to document disclosures of Protected Health Information and information related to such disclosures as would be required for Covered Entity to respond to a request by an Individual for an accounting of disclosure of Protected Health Information in accordance with 45 CFR § 164.528.

2.10 Business Associate agrees to provide Covered Entity or an Individual, in time and manner designated by Covered Entity, information collected in accordance with this Agreement, to permit Covered Entity to respond to a request by an Individual for and accounting of disclosures of Protected Health Information in accordance with 45 CFR § 164.528, provided that Business Associate shall have at least twenty (20) days from Covered Entity notice to provide access to, or deliver, such information which shall include, at minimum, (a) date of the disclosure; (b) name of the third party to whom the Protected Health Information was disclosed and, if known, the address of the third party; (c) brief description of the disclosed information; and (d) brief explanation of the purpose and basis for such disclosure.

2.11 Business Associate agrees it must limit any use, disclosure, or request for use or disclosure of Protected Health Information to the minimum amount necessary to accomplish the intended purpose of the use, disclosure, or request in accordance with the requirements of the Privacy Rule.

2.11.1 Business Associate represents to Covered Entity that all its uses and disclosures of, or requests for, Protected Health Information shall be the minimum necessary in accordance with the Privacy Rule requirements.

2.11.2 Covered Entity may, pursuant to the Privacy Rule, reasonably rely on any requested disclosure as the minimum necessary for the stated purpose when the information is requested by Business Associate.

2.11.3 Business Associate acknowledges that if Business Associate is also a covered entity, as defined by the Privacy Rule, Business Associate is required, independent of Business Associate's obligations under this Memorandum, to comply with the Privacy Rule's minimum necessary requirements when making any request for Protected Health Information from Covered Entity.

2.12 Business Associate agrees to adequately and properly maintain all Protected Health Information received from, or created, or received on behalf of, Covered Entity.

2.13 If Business Associate receives a request from an Individual for a copy of the individual's Protected Health Information, and the Protected Health Information is in the sole possession of the Business Associate, Business Associate will provide the requested copies to the individual and notify the Covered Entity of such action. If Business Associate receives a request for Protected Health Information in the possession of the Covered Entity, or receives a request to exercise other individual rights as set forth in the Privacy Rule, Business Associate shall notify Covered Entity of such request and forward the request to Covered Entity. Business Associate shall then assist Covered Entity in responding to the request.

2.14 Business Associate agrees to fully cooperate in good faith with and to assist Covered Entity in complying with the requirements of the Privacy Rule.

3 OBLIGATIONS AND ACTIVITIES OF BUSINESS ASSOCIATE (Security Rule)

3.1 Business Associate agrees to fully comply with the requirements under the Security Rule applicable to "business associates," as that term is defined in the Security Rule. In case of any conflict between this Agreement and Service Agreements, this Agreement shall govern.

3.2 Business Associate agrees to implement administrative, physical, and technical safeguards that reasonably and appropriately protect the confidentiality, integrity, and availability of the electronic protected health information that it creates, receives, maintains, or transmits on behalf of the covered entity as required by the Security Rule.

3.3 Business Associate shall ensure that any agent, including a subcontractor, to whom it provides electronic protected health information received from or created for Covered Entity or that carries out any duties for the Business Associate involving the use, custody, disclosure, creation of, or access to Protected Health Information supplied by Covered Entity, to agree, by written contract (or the appropriate equivalent if the agent is a government entity) with Business Associate, to the same restrictions and conditions that apply through this Agreement to Business Associate with respect to such information.

3.4   Business Associate agrees to require its employees, agents, and subcontractors to report to Business Associate within five (5) business days, any Security Incident (as that term is defined in 45 CFR Section 164.304) of which it becomes aware. Business Associate agrees to promptly report any Security Incident of which it becomes aware to Covered Entity.

3.5   Business Associate agrees to make its internal practices, books, and records (including policies and procedures relating to the security of electronic protected health information) received from, created by, or received by Business Associate on behalf of Covered Entity available to the Secretary of the United States Department of Health and Human Services or the Secretary's designee, in a time and manner designated by the Secretary, for purposes of determining Covered Entity's or Business Associate's compliance with the Security Rule.

3.6   Business Associate agrees to fully cooperate in good faith with and to assist Covered Entity in complying with the requirements of the Security Rule.

4.   PERMITTED USES AND DISCLOSURES BY BUSINESS ASSOCIATE

4.1   Except as otherwise limited in this Agreement, Business Associate may use or disclose Protected Health Information to perform functions, activities, or services for, or on behalf of, Covered Entity as specified in Service Contracts, provided that such use or disclosure would not violate the Privacy and Security Rule, if done by Covered Entity.

4.2   Except as otherwise limited in this Agreement, Business Associate may use Protected Health Information as required for Business Associate's proper management and administration or to carry out the legal responsibilities of the Business Associate.

4.3   Except as otherwise limited in this Agreement, Business Associate may disclose Protected Health Information for the proper management and administration of the Business Associate, provided that disclosures are required by law, or provided that, if Business Associate discloses any Protected Health Information to a third party for such a purpose, Business Associate shall enter into a written agreement with such third party requiring the third party to: (a) maintain the confidentiality, integrity, and availability of Protected Health Information and not to use or further disclose such information except as required by law or for the purpose for which it was disclosed, and (b) notify Business Associate of any instances in which it becomes aware that the confidentiality, integrity, and/or availability of the Protected Health Information is breached.

4.4   Except as otherwise limited in this Agreement, Business Associate may use Protected Health Information to provide Data Aggregation services to Covered Entity as permitted by 42 CFR § 164.504(e)(2)(I)(B).

4.5   Business Associate may use Protected Health Information to report violations of law to appropriate federal and state authorities consistent with 45 CFR 164.502(j)(1)

5.   OBLIGATIONS OF COVERED ENTITY

5.1   Covered Entity shall provide Business Associate with the notice of Privacy Practices that Covered Entity produces in accordance with 45 CFR § 164.520, as well as any changes to such notice. Covered Entity shall notify Business Associate of any limitations in its notice that affect Business Associate's use or disclosure of Protected Health Information.

5.2   Covered Entity shall provide Business Associate with any changes in, or revocation of, permission by an Individual to use or disclose Protected Health Information, if such changes affect Business Associate's permitted or required uses.

5.3   Covered Entity shall notify Business Associate of any restriction to the use or disclosure of Protected Health Information that Covered Entity has agreed to in accordance with 45 CFR § 164.522, to the extent that such restriction may affect Business Associate's use of Protected Health Information.

6.   PERMISSIBLE REQUESTS BY COVERED ENTITY

6.1   Covered Entity shall not request Business Associate to use or disclose Protected Health Information in any manner that would not be permissible under the Privacy or Security Rule, if done by Covered Entity.

7.   TERM AND TERMINATION

7.1   Term. This Agreement shall be effective as of the date on which it is signed by both parties and shall terminate when all of the Protected Health Information provided by Covered Entity to Business Associate, or created or received by Business Associate on behalf of Covered Entity, is destroyed or returned to Covered Entity, or, if it is infeasible to return or destroy Protected Health Information, Section 7.3. below shall apply.

7.2   Termination for Cause

7.2.1.   This Agreement authorizes and Business Associate acknowledges and agrees Covered Entity shall have the right to immediately terminate this Agreement and Service Contracts in the event Business Associate fails to comply with, or violates a material provision of, requirements of the Privacy and/or Security Rule or this Memorandum.

7.2.2.   Upon Covered Entity's knowledge of a material breach by Business Associate, Covered Entity shall either:

7.2.2.1.   provide a reasonable opportunity for Business Associate to cure the breach or end the violation or

7.2.2.2.   if Business Associate has breached a material term of this Agreement and cure is not possible or if Business Associate does not cure a curable breach or end the violation within a reasonable time as specified by, and at the sole discretion of, Covered Entity, Covered Entity may immediately terminate this Agreement and the Service Agreement.

7.2.2.3.   If neither cure nor termination is feasible, Covered Entity shall report the violation to the Secretary of the United States Department of Health and Human Services or the Secretary's designee.

7.3.   Effect of Termination.

7.3.1.   Except as provided in Section 7.3.2. below, upon termination of this Agreement, for any reason, Business Associate shall return or destroy all Protected Health Information received from Covered Entity, or created or received by Business Associate on behalf of, Covered Entity. This provision shall apply to Protected Health Information that is in the possession of subcontractors or agents of Business Associate. Business Associate shall retain no copies of the Protected Health Information.

7.3.2.   In the event that Business Associate determines that returning or destroying the Protected Health Information is not feasible, Business Associate shall provide to Covered Entity notification of the conditions that make return or destruction unfeasible. Upon mutual agreement of the Parties that return or destruction of Protected Health Information is unfeasible, Business Associate shall extend the protections of this Memorandum to such Protected Health Information and limit further uses and disclosures of such Protected Health Information to those purposes that make the return or destruction unfeasible, for so long as Business Associate maintains such Protected Health Information.

8. MISCELLANEOUS

8.1 <u>Regulatory Reference</u>. A reference in this Agreement to a section in the Privacy and/or Security Rule means the section as in effect or as amended.

8.2 <u>Amendment</u>. The Parties agree to take such action as is necessary to amend this Memorandum from time to time as is necessary for Covered Entity to comply with the requirements of the Privacy and Security Rules and the Health Insurance Portability and Accountability Act, Public Law 104-191. Business Associate and Covered Entity shall comply with any amendment to the Privacy and Security Rules, the Health Insurance Portability and Accountability Act, Public Law 104-191, and related regulations upon the effective date of such amendment, regardless of whether this Agreement has been formally amended.

8.3 <u>Survival</u>. The respective rights and obligations of Business Associate under Section 7.3. of this Memorandum shall survive the termination of this Agreement.

8.4 <u>Interpretation</u>. Any ambiguity in this Agreement shall be resolved in favor of a meaning that permits Covered Entity and the Business Associate to comply with the Privacy and Security Rules.

8.5 <u>Notices and Communications</u>. All instructions, notices, consents, demands, or other communications required or contemplated by this Agreement shall be in writing and shall be delivered by hand, by facsimile transmission, by overnight courier service, or by first class mail, postage prepaid, addressed to the respective party at the appropriate facsimile number or address as set forth below, or to such other party, facsimile number, or address as may be hereafter specified by written notice.

COVERED ENTITY:	BUSINESS ASSOCIATE:
State Name	
Project Director	**BUSINESS ASSOCIATE NAME**
Department of Finance and	**NAME AND TITLE**
Administration	**ADDRESS**
ADDRESS	Telephone: **NUMBER**
Capitol City, NY 12345	Fax: **NUMBER**
Phone:	
Fax:	

All instructions, notices, consents, demands, or other communications shall be considered effectively given as of the date of hand delivery; as of the date specified for overnight courier service delivery; as of three (3) business days after the date of mailing; or on the day the facsimile transmission is received mechanically by the facsimile machine at the receiving location and receipt is verbally confirmed by the sender.

8.6 <u>Strict Compliance</u>. No failure by any Party to insist upon strict compliance with any term or provision of this Agreement, to exercise any option, to enforce any right, or to seek any remedy upon any default of any other Party shall affect, or constitute a waiver of, any Party's right to insist upon such strict compliance, exercise that option, enforce that right, or seek that remedy with respect to that default or any prior, contemporaneous, or subsequent default. No custom or practice of the Parties at variance with any provision of this Agreement shall affect, or constitute a waiver of, any Party's right to demand strict compliance with all provisions of this Agreement.

8.7 <u>Severability</u>. With respect to any provision of this Agreement finally determined by a court of competent jurisdiction to be unenforceable, such court shall have jurisdiction to reform such provision so that it is enforceable to the maximum extent permitted by applicable law, and the Parties shall abide by such court's determination. In the event that any provision of this Agreement cannot be reformed, such provision shall be deemed severed from this Agreement, but every other provision of this Agreement shall remain in full force and effect.

8.8 <u>Governing Law</u>. This Agreement shall be governed by and construed in accordance with the laws of the State Government except to the extent that State law has been preempted by HIPAA.

8.9 <u>Compensation</u>. There shall be **no** remuneration for performance under this Agreement except as specifically provided by, in, and through, existing administrative requirements, State government requirements, and services contracts referenced herein.

IN WITNESS WHEREOF,

_____ **Date:**

_____ **Date:**

PROPOSAL TRANSMITTAL AND STATEMENT OF CERTIFICATIONS AND ASSURANCES

The Proposer must complete and sign this *Proposal Transmittal and Statement of Certifications and Assurances*. It must be signed, in the space below, by an individual empowered to bind the proposing entity to the provisions of this RFP and any contract awarded pursuant to it. If said individual is not the Proposer's chief executive or president, this document shall attach evidence showing the individual's authority to bind the proposing entity.

Any contract resulting from this RFP process shall incorporate this *Proposal Transmittal and Statement of Certifications and Assurances* by reference as a part of said contract (refer to *pro forma* contract "Special Terms and Conditions").

PROPOSER LEGAL ENTITY NAME:

PROPOSER FEDERAL EMPLOYER IDENTIFICATION NUMBER:
(or Social Security Number)

The Proposer does hereby affirm and expressly declare confirmation, certification, and assurance of the following:

1) This proposal constitutes a commitment to provide all services as defined in the RFP Attachment 6.1, *Pro Forma* Contract Scope of Services for the total contract period and confirmation that the Proposer shall comply with all of the provisions in this RFP and shall accept all terms and conditions set out in the RFP Attachment 6.1, *Pro Forma* Contract.

2) The information detailed in the proposal submitted herewith in response to the subject RFP is accurate.

3) The proposal submitted herewith in response to the subject RFP shall remain valid for at least 120 days subsequent to the date of the Cost Proposal opening and thereafter in accordance with any contract pursuant to the RFP.

4) The Proposers shall comply with:

   a) the laws of the State Government;

   b) Title VI of the federal Civil Rights Act of 1964;

   c) Title IX of the federal Education Amendments Act of 1972;

   d) the Equal Employment Opportunity Act and the regulations issued there under by the federal government;

   e) the Americans with Disabilities Act of 1990 and the regulations issued there under by the federal government;

   f) the condition that the submitted proposal was independently arrived at, without collusion, under penalty of perjury; and,

   g) the condition that no amount shall be paid directly or indirectly to an employee or official of the State Government as wages, compensation, or gifts in exchange for acting as an officer, agent, employee, subcontractor, or consultant to the Proposer in connection with the Procurement under this RFP.

SIGNATURE & DATE:

TECHNICAL PROPOSAL & EVALUATION GUIDE — SECTION A

PROPOSER NAME:	

SECTION A — MANDATORY REQUIREMENTS

The Proposer must address ALL Mandatory Requirements section items and provide, in sequence, the information and documentation as required (referenced with the associated item references). The RFP Coordinator will review all general mandatory requirements, including but not limited to the following:

- Proposal received on or before the Proposal Deadline
- Technical Proposal copies and Cost Proposal packaged separately
- Technical Proposal contains NO cost data
- Proposer did NOT submit alternate proposals
- Proposer did NOT submit multiple proposals in a different form
- Technical Proposal does NOT contain any restrictions of the rights of the State or other qualification of the proposal

The RFP Coordinator will also review the proposal to determine if the Mandatory Requirement Items (below) are met and mark each with pass or fail. For each requirement that is not met, the Proposal Evaluation Team must review the proposal and attach a written determination.

Any contract resulting from this RFP process shall incorporate by reference the respective proposal responses to all items below as a part of said contract (refer to *pro forma* contract "Special Terms and Conditions").

NOTICE: In addition to these requirements, the State will also evaluate compliance with ALL RFP requirements.

Proposal Page # (to be completed by Proposer)	Mandatory Requirement Items	State Use ONLY Pass/Fail
	A.1 Provide the Proposal Transmittal and Statement of Certifications and Assurances (detailed in RFP Attachment 6.2) completed and signed, in the space provided, by an individual empowered to bind the Proposer to the provisions of this RFP and any resulting contract. *Each Proposer **must** sign the Proposal Transmittal and Statement of Certifications and Assurances without exception or qualification.*	

	A.2	Provide the following as documentation of financial responsibility and stability:	
		<ul><li>a current written bank reference, in the form of a standard business letter, indicating that the proposer's business relationship with the financial institution is in positive standing</li><li>two current written, positive credit references, in the form of standard business letters, from vendors with which the Proposer has done business or a positive credit rating determined by a accredited credit bureau within the last 6 months and the associated credit report number; inclusion of the credit report number without the actual credit rating is insufficient</li><li>a copy of a valid certificate of insurance indicating liability insurance in the amount of at least One Million Dollars ($1,000,000)</li></ul>	
	A.3	Provide a statement of whether the Proposer or any individual who shall perform work under the contract has a possible conflict of interest (*e.g.,* employment by the State Government) and, if so, the nature of that conflict. ***Any questions of conflict of interest shall be solely within the discretion of the State, and the State reserves the right to cancel any award.***	
	A.4	Provide a statement confirming that the Proposer does **not** have active managed-security service provider contract(s) with any State Government agency.	
	A.5	The Proposer must have performed a vulnerability assessment and/or penetration test on a government entity or corporation that has the minimum of 5,000 employees. **Evidence of this should be in the form of a list of the Proposer's clients meeting this requirement with the total number of employees for each client identified with the client name**. The employee count should be the **total** number of employees in the **entire** organization (federal agency, state government, county government, corporation, etc.), including all divisions, agencies, sections, etc., and may be rounded to the nearest hundred. (For example, the State Government has approximately 40,000 employees.)	

TECHNICAL PROPOSAL & EVALUATION GUIDE — SECTION B

PROPOSER NAME:	

SECTION B — QUALIFICATIONS & EXPERIENCE

The Proposer must address ALL Qualifications and Experience section items and provide, in sequence, the information and documentation as required (referenced with the associated item references).

A Proposal Evaluation Team, made up of three or more State employees, will independently evaluate and score the proposal's "qualifications and experience" responses.

Any contract resulting from this RFP process shall incorporate by reference the respective proposal responses to all items below as a part of said contract (refer to *pro forma* contract "Special Terms and Conditions").

Proposal Page # (to be completed by Proposer)		Qualifications & Experience Items
	B.1	Describe the Proposer's form of business (*i.e.*, individual, sole proprietor, corporation, nonprofit corporation, partnership, limited liability company) and detail the name, mailing address, and telephone number of the person the State should contact regarding the proposal.
	B.2	Provide a statement of whether there have been any mergers, acquisitions, or sales of the Proposer company within the last ten years, and if so, an explanation providing relevant details.
	B.3	Provide a statement of whether the Proposer or any of the Proposer's employees, agents, independent contractors, or subcontractors have been convicted of, pled guilty to, or pled *nolo contendere* to any felony, and if so, an explanation providing relevant details.
	B.4	Provide a statement of whether there is any pending litigation against the Proposer; and if such litigation exists, an attached opinion of counsel as to whether the pending litigation will impair the Proposer's performance in a contract under this RFP.
	B.5	Provide a statement of whether, in the last ten years, the Proposer has filed (or had filed against it) any bankruptcy or insolvency proceeding, whether voluntary or involuntary, or undergone the appointment of a receiver, trustee, or assignee for the benefit of creditors, and if so, an explanation providing relevant details.
	B.6	Provide a statement of whether there are any pending Securities Exchange Commission investigations involving the Proposer, and if such are pending or in progress, an explanation providing relevant details and an attached opinion of counsel as to whether the pending investigation(s) will impair the Proposer's performance in a contract under this RFP.
	B.7	Provide a brief, descriptive statement indicating the Proposer's credentials to deliver the services sought under this RFP.
	B.8	Briefly describe how long the Proposer has been performing the services required by this RFP and include the number of years in business.
	B.9	Describe the Proposer organization's number of employees, client base, and location of offices.

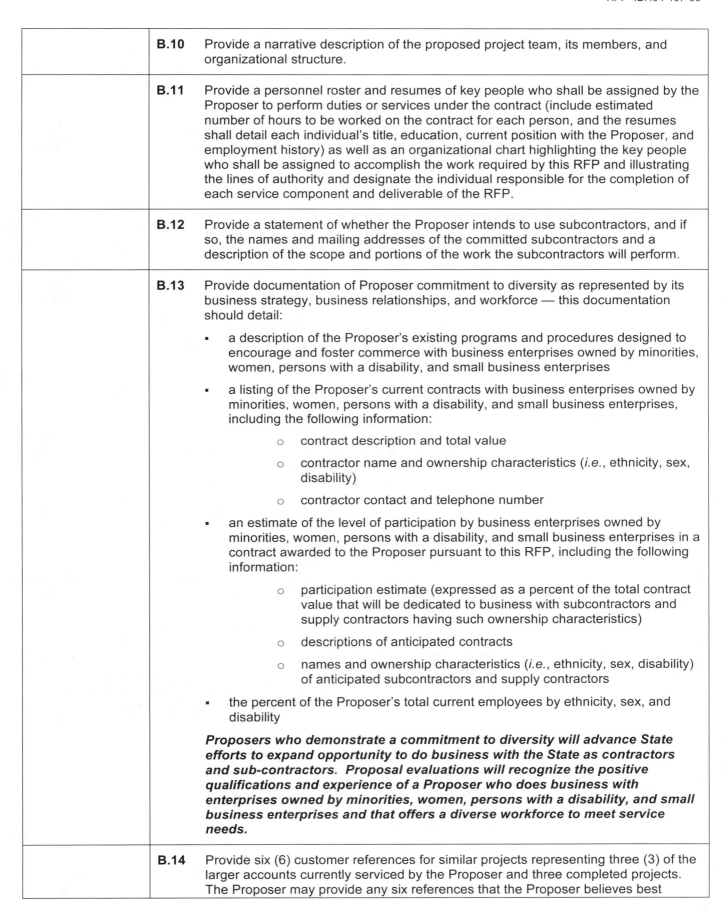

	B.10	Provide a narrative description of the proposed project team, its members, and organizational structure.
	B.11	Provide a personnel roster and resumes of key people who shall be assigned by the Proposer to perform duties or services under the contract (include estimated number of hours to be worked on the contract for each person, and the resumes shall detail each individual's title, education, current position with the Proposer, and employment history) as well as an organizational chart highlighting the key people who shall be assigned to accomplish the work required by this RFP and illustrating the lines of authority and designate the individual responsible for the completion of each service component and deliverable of the RFP.
	B.12	Provide a statement of whether the Proposer intends to use subcontractors, and if so, the names and mailing addresses of the committed subcontractors and a description of the scope and portions of the work the subcontractors will perform.
	B.13	Provide documentation of Proposer commitment to diversity as represented by its business strategy, business relationships, and workforce — this documentation should detail: <ul><li>a description of the Proposer's existing programs and procedures designed to encourage and foster commerce with business enterprises owned by minorities, women, persons with a disability, and small business enterprises</li><li>a listing of the Proposer's current contracts with business enterprises owned by minorities, women, persons with a disability, and small business enterprises, including the following information:<ul><li>contract description and total value</li><li>contractor name and ownership characteristics (*i.e.*, ethnicity, sex, disability)</li><li>contractor contact and telephone number</li></ul></li><li>an estimate of the level of participation by business enterprises owned by minorities, women, persons with a disability, and small business enterprises in a contract awarded to the Proposer pursuant to this RFP, including the following information:<ul><li>participation estimate (expressed as a percent of the total contract value that will be dedicated to business with subcontractors and supply contractors having such ownership characteristics)</li><li>descriptions of anticipated contracts</li><li>names and ownership characteristics (*i.e.*, ethnicity, sex, disability) of anticipated subcontractors and supply contractors</li></ul></li><li>the percent of the Proposer's total current employees by ethnicity, sex, and disability</li></ul> ***Proposers who demonstrate a commitment to diversity will advance State efforts to expand opportunity to do business with the State as contractors and sub-contractors. Proposal evaluations will recognize the positive qualifications and experience of a Proposer who does business with enterprises owned by minorities, women, persons with a disability, and small business enterprises and that offers a diverse workforce to meet service needs.***
	B.14	Provide six (6) customer references for similar projects representing three (3) of the larger accounts currently serviced by the Proposer and three completed projects. The Proposer may provide any six references that the Proposer believes best

address the requirements stated above. However, the Proposer may **NOT** provide more than six references for the Proposer in its response. If the Proposer provides more than six Proposer references in response to this Section B.14, the State will **randomly** select six for evaluation purposes.

The Proposer should also include at least one reference for each of the Proposer's proposed subcontractors, if any. If the Proposer has any State Government references, the Proposer may submit these as well, using the same process described herein. Subcontractor and State Government references are not included in the six-reference limit described above; subcontractor and State Government references are in addition to the six-reference limit described above.

All references shall be provided to the State in the form of questionnaires that have been fully completed by the individual providing the reference. The State has included the reference check questionnaire to be used, as RFP Attachment 6.6. **THE PROPOSER MUST USE THIS FORM, OR AN EXACT DUPLICATE THEREOF.**

The Proposer will be solely responsible for obtaining the fully completed reference check questionnaires, and for including them within the Proposer's sealed Technical Proposal. In order to obtain and submit the completed reference check questionnaire, the Proposer shall follow the process detailed below exactly:

1. Proposer makes an exact duplicate of the State's form, as it appears in RFP Attachment 6.6.

2. Proposer sends the copy of the form to the reference it has chosen, along with a new, standard #10 envelope.

3. Proposer directs the person providing the reference check feedback to complete the form in its entirety, sign and date it, and seal it within the provided envelope. The person may prepare a manual document or complete the exact duplicate Word document and print the completed copy for submission. After sealing the envelope, the person providing the reference must sign his or her name in ink across the sealed portion of the envelope and return it directly to the Proposer. The Proposer will give the reference check provider a deadline, such that the Proposer will be able to collect all references in time to include them within its sealed Technical Proposal.

4. When the Proposer receives the sealed envelopes from the reference check providers, the Proposer **will not open** them. Instead, the Proposer will enclose all of the unopened reference check envelopes, in an easily identifiable larger envelope, and will include this envelope as a part of the written Technical Proposal. Therefore, when the State opens the Technical Proposal box, the State will find a clearly labeled envelope enclosed, which contains all of the sealed reference check envelopes.

5. The State will base its reference check evaluation on the contents of these envelopes. **THE STATE WILL NOT ACCEPT LATE REFERENCES OR REFERENCES SUBMITTED THROUGH ANY OTHER CHANNEL OF SUBMISSION OR MEDIUM, WHETHER WRITTEN, ELECTRONIC, VERBAL, OR OTHERWISE.**

Each reference must include:

- The Proposer's name
- The reference's organization name
- The name of the person responding
- The title of person responding
- The date the reference form was completed

6. The State reserves the right to clarify information presented in the reference check questionnaires, and may consider clarification responses in the evaluation

		of reference checks. However, the State is under no obligation to clarify any reference check information. *Each evaluator will generally consider the references provided in accordance with the rules above. Current or prior contracts with the State are not a prerequisite and are not required for the maximum evaluation score possible, and the existence of such contracts with the State will not automatically result in the addition or deduction of evaluation points.*
	B.15	Provide a list, if any, of all current contracts with the State Government and all those completed within the previous five-year period. This list must include: • The procuring State agency • A brief description of the contract's scope of services • The contract number • The contract term *Current or prior contracts with the State are not a prerequisite and are not required for the maximum evaluation score possible, and the existence of such contracts with the State will not automatically result in the addition or deduction of evaluation points.*
	(Maximum Section B Score =30)	
	SCORE *(for all Section B items above, B.1 through B.15)*:	

TECHNICAL PROPOSAL & EVALUATION GUIDE — SECTION C

PROPOSER NAME:	

SECTION C — TECHNICAL APPROACH

The Proposer must address ALL Technical Approach section items and provide, in sequence, the information and documentation as required (referenced with the associated item references). A Proposal Evaluation Team, made up of three or more State employees, will independently evaluate and score the proposal's response to each item. Each evaluator will use the following whole number, raw point scale for scoring each item:

0 = little value	1 = poor	2 = fair	3 = satisfactory	4 = good	5 = excellent

The RFP Coordinator will multiply each item score by the assigned weight with the product being the item's raw weighted score for purposes of calculating the section score as detailed at the end of this table.

Any contract resulting from this RFP process shall incorporate by reference the respective proposal responses to all items below as a part of said contract (refer to *pro forma* contract "Special Terms and Conditions").

Proposal Page # (to be completed by Proposer)		Technical Approach Items	State Use ONLY		
			Score	Item Weight	Raw Weighted Score
	C.1	Provide a narrative that illustrates the Proposer's understanding of the State's requirements and project schedule.		3	
	C.2	Provide a narrative that illustrates how the Proposer will complete the scope of services, accomplish required objectives, and meet the State's project schedule.		4	
	C.3	Provide a narrative that illustrates how the Proposer will manage the project, ensure completion of the scope of services, and accomplish required objectives within the State's project schedule.		4	
	C.4	Provide a narrative illustrating your methodology for conducting vulnerability assessments and penetration tests.		3	
	C.5	Provide a narrative describing how you apply your vulnerability assessment and penetration testing methodologies in performing the services for customers. Including: project management, incident and emergency procedures, findings, vulnerabilities, and/or report delivery practices.		5	
	C.6	Provide a narrative detailing the systems that you are able to assess for vulnerabilities. Including but not limited to: operating systems, databases, applications, and infrastructure/networking.		3	
	C.7	Provide a narrative illustrating your methodology for reviewing code.		3	

	C.8	Provide a narrative describing how you apply your code review methodologies in performing the services for customers. Including project management, incident and emergency procedures, findings, vulnerabilities, and/or report delivery practices.	**5**	
	C.9	Provide a list of the code languages you can review.	**3**	
	C.10	Provide an anonymous example of a report outlining the required deliverables as provided in the Scope of Services.	**4**	
	C.11	Please provide a narrative describing your process for conducting background checks on your employees.	**3**	

Total Raw Weighted Score: *(sum of Raw Weighted Scores above)*		

Total Raw Weighted Score ───────────────── **maximum possible raw weighted score** *(i.e., 5 x the sum of item weights above)*	**X40** *(maximum section score)*	**= SCORE:**	

TECHNICAL PROPOSAL & EVALUATION GUIDE — SECTION D

PROPOSER NAME:

SECTION D — SECURITY GAP ANALYSIS

The Proposer must address ALL Security Gap Analysis section items and provide, in sequence, the information and documentation as required (referenced with the associated item references). A Proposal Evaluation Team, made up of three or more State employees, will independently evaluate and score the proposal's response to each item. Each evaluator will use the following whole number, raw point scale for scoring each item:

0 = little value   *1 = poor*   *2 = fair*   *3 = satisfactory*   *4 = good*   *5 = excellent*

The RFP Coordinator will multiply each item score by the assigned weight with the product being the item's raw weighted score for purposes of calculating the section score as detailed at the end of this table.

Any contract resulting from this RFP process shall incorporate by reference the respective proposal responses to all items below as a part of said contract (refer to *pro forma* contract "Special Terms and Conditions").

Proposal Page # (to be completed by Proposer)	Technical Approach Items	State Use ONLY		
		Score	Item Weight	Raw Weighted Score
	D.1 Provide a narrative describing your approach for performing an IT Security Policy Framework gap analysis.		5	
	D.2 Describe your approach for ensuring IT security policies are in compliance with HIPAA requirements.		3	
	D.3 Describe your approach for ensuring IT security policies are in compliance with PCI DSS requirements.		3	
	D.4 Provide a narrative for how you will define and implement new policies ensuring State Government Privacy Laws for protecting citizen privacy data.		4	
	D.5 Provide a narrative describing how you will define and implement administrative controls to ensure the state's AUP is effectively communicated and enforced.		4	
	D.6 Describe your approach for ensuring the State's network traffic is monitored and examined prior to leaving any ingress/egress point – preventing data leakage or loss of confidential data – what policies are needed to support this requirements?		3	
	D.7 Provide a narrative describing how the State can ensure change management is performed in a controlled manner with full documentation and prior authorization requirements.		4	

	D.8	Identify any gaps in the current access control policy definition to ensure remote users, mobile users, and workers from home maintain confidentiality of remote data access. Describe your recommendations for remediating any identified gaps.	4	
	D.9	Describe your approach for defining policies needed for a Business Continuity Plan and Disaster Recovery Plan. How can you help the State define and implement these policies?	4	
	D.10	Given the State's existing IT security policy framework, describe what gaps were identified and how you intend to fill them. Recommend policies that are needed to fill identified gaps. Describe how you intend to implement them statewide.	5	

Total Raw Weighted Score: *(sum of Raw Weighted Scores above)*	

Total Raw Weighted Score ─────────────────────────────── **maximum possible raw weighted score** *(i.e., 5 x the sum of item weights above)*	**X40** *(maximum section score)*	**= SCORE:**

TECHNICAL PROPOSAL & EVALUATION GUIDE — SECTION E

PROPOSER NAME:	

SECTION E — PRIVACY DATA

The Proposer must address ALL Privacy Data section items and provide, in sequence, the information and documentation as required (referenced with the associated item references). A Proposal Evaluation Team, made up of three or more State employees, will independently evaluate and score the proposal's response to each item. Each evaluator will use the following whole number, raw point scale for scoring each item:

0 = little value	1 = poor	2 = fair	3 = satisfactory	4 = good	5 = excellent

The RFP Coordinator will multiply each item score by the assigned weight with the product being the item's raw weighted score for purposes of calculating the section score as detailed at the end of this table.

Any contract resulting from this RFP process shall incorporate by reference the respective proposal responses to all items below as a part of said contract (refer to *pro forma* contract "Special Terms and Conditions").

Proposal Page # (to be completed by Proposer)	Technical Approach Items	State Use ONLY		
		Score	Item Weight	Raw Weighted Score
	E.1 Provide a narrative describing your approach for reviewing compliance requirements for privacy data.		4	
	E.2 Describe your approach for reviewing state laws, policies, and data classification standards as they pertain to handling and protecting privacy data.		4	
	E.3 Describe your approach for ensuring IT security policies are in compliance with all applicable privacy data requirements.		5	
	E.4 Provide a narrative for how you will review and assess existing controls that protecting citizen privacy data.		4	
	E.5 Describe your approach for identifying gaps in control coverage for protecting privacy data.		5	
	E.6 Provide a narrative describing how the State can fill each of the identified compliance gaps in protecting privacy data.		6	
	E.7 Describe your approach for defining policies needed to address compliance gaps for privacy data protection.		6	
	E.8 Provide a narrative for how you will define and implement new policies ensuring State Government Privacy Laws for protecting citizen privacy data.		6	

Total Raw Weighted Score: *(sum of Raw Weighted Scores above)*	

Total Raw Weighted Score ――――――――――――――――――― **maximum possible raw weighted score** *(i.e., 5 x the sum of item weights above)*	**X40** *(maximum section score)*	**= SCORE:**	

TECHNICAL PROPOSAL & EVALUATION GUIDE — SECTION F

PROPOSER NAME:	

SECTION F —SECURITY ASSESSMENT

The Proposer must address ALL Security Assessment section items and provide, in sequence, the information and documentation as required (referenced with the associated item references). A Proposal Evaluation Team, made up of three or more State employees, will independently evaluate and score the proposal's response to each item. Each evaluator will use the following whole number, raw point scale for scoring each item:

0 = little value	*1 = poor*	*2 = fair*	*3 = satisfactory*	*4 = good*	*5 = excellent*

The RFP Coordinator will multiply each item score by the assigned weight with the product being the item's raw weighted score for purposes of calculating the section score as detailed at the end of this table.

Any contract resulting from this RFP process shall incorporate by reference the respective proposal responses to all items below as a part of said contract (refer to *pro forma* contract "Special Terms and Conditions").

Proposal Page # (to be completed by Proposer)	Technical Approach Items	State Use ONLY		
		Score	Item Weight	Raw Weighted Score
	F.1 Provide a narrative describing your approach for identifying and assessing risks, threats, and vulnerabilities in the seven domains of the typical IT infrastructure.		4	
	F.2 Describe your approach for reviewing existing policies and controls in each of the seven domains in the IT infrastructure.		4	
	F.3 Provide a narrative for how you will develop a list of known risks, threats, and vulnerabilities that exist for components in the current IT infrastructure.		5	
	F.4 Describe your approach for assessing IT infrastructure components to identify security risks, threats, and vulnerabilities in each of the seven domains.		4	
	F.5 Describe your approach for preparing a list of identified security risks, threats, and vulnerabilities in each of the seven domains of a typical IT infrastructure.		5	
	F.6 Provide a narrative describing how to prioritize the identified security risks, threats, and vulnerabilities in each of the seven domains, and for the overall IT environment.		6	
	F.7 Describe your approach for preparing a formal assessment report that explains each of the identified security risks, threats, and vulnerabilities		6	

	for the seven domains in the typical IT infrastructure.			
	F.8 Provide a narrative for how you will organize the assessment report to provide an executive summary and a prioritized list of security risks, threats, and vulnerabilities in the seven domains of the typical IT infrastructure.		6	

Total Raw Weighted Score: *(sum of Raw Weighted Scores above)*	

Total Raw Weighted Score ————————————————— **maximum possible raw weighted score** *(i.e., 5 x the sum of item weights above)*	**X40** *(maximum section score)*	**= SCORE:**	

TECHNICAL PROPOSAL & EVALUATION GUIDE — SECTION G

PROPOSER NAME:	

SECTION G —SECURITY ASSESSMENT REPORT

The Proposer must address ALL Security Assessment Report section items and provide, in sequence, the information and documentation as required (referenced with the associated item references). A Proposal Evaluation Team, made up of three or more State employees, will independently evaluate and score the proposal's response to each item. Each evaluator will use the following whole number, raw point scale for scoring each item:

0 = little value	1 = poor	2 = fair	3 = satisfactory	4 = good	5 = excellent

The RFP Coordinator will multiply each item score by the assigned weight with the product being the item's raw weighted score for purposes of calculating the section score as detailed at the end of this table.

Any contract resulting from this RFP process shall incorporate by reference the respective proposal responses to all items below as a part of said contract (refer to *pro forma* contract "Special Terms and Conditions").

Proposal Page # (to be completed by Proposer)	Technical Approach Items	State Use ONLY		
		Score	Item Weight	Raw Weighted Score
	G.1 Provide a narrative describing your approach for prioritizing and summarizing identified risks, threats, and vulnerabilities in the seven domains of the typical IT infrastructure.		4	
	G.2 Describe your approach for preparing a qualitative risk assessment for the IT infrastructure described in this RFP's technical description.		4	
	G.3 Provide a narrative for how you will identify the highest priority resources to include in a qualitative risk assessment for each IT domain.		5	
	G.4 Describe your approach for identifying risks and impact for all identified resources across the seven domains of the IT infrastructure.		4	
	G.5 Describe your approach for prioritizing each risk by severity and impact, both in the context of individual domains and over the entire IT infrastructure.		5	
	G.6 Provide a narrative describing how to identify the most appropriate response to each risk, prioritized by effectiveness and ROI.		6	
	G.7 Describe your approach for preparing a formal qualitative risk assessment report that explains each of the identified risks across the seven domains of a typical IT infrastructure and the recommended responses to each risk.		6	

| | G.8 | Provide a narrative for how you will organize the qualitative assessment report to provide an executive summary and a prioritized list of risks to resources and recommended responses to each risk. | | 6 | |

| | **Total Raw Weighted Score:** *(sum of Raw Weighted Scores above)* | |

| **Total Raw Weighted Score** ─────────────────────── **maximum possible raw weighted score** *(i.e., 5 x the sum of item weights above)* | **X40** *(maximum section score)* | **= SCORE:** | |

TECHNICAL PROPOSAL & EVALUATION GUIDE — SECTION H

PROPOSER NAME:	

SECTION H —MITIGATING RISKS

The Proposer must address ALL Mitigating Risks section items and provide, in sequence, the information and documentation as required (referenced with the associated item references). A Proposal Evaluation Team, made up of three or more State employees, will independently evaluate and score the proposal's response to each item. Each evaluator will use the following whole number, raw point scale for scoring each item:

0 = *little value*	1 = *poor*	2 = *fair*	3 = *satisfactory*	4 = *good*	5 = *excellent*

The RFP Coordinator will multiply each item score by the assigned weight with the product being the item's raw weighted score for purposes of calculating the section score as detailed at the end of this table.

Any contract resulting from this RFP process shall incorporate by reference the respective proposal responses to all items below as a part of said contract (refer to *pro forma* contract "Special Terms and Conditions").

Proposal Page # (to be completed by Proposer)	Technical Approach Items	State Use ONLY		
		Score	Item Weight	Raw Weighted Score
	H.1 Provide a narrative describing your approach for using the qualitative risk assessment report to direct mitigation efforts.		5	
	H.2 Describe your approach for preparing a prioritized risk response report based on the information and recommendations in the qualitative risk assessment report.		5	
	H.3 Provide a narrative for how you will determine which of the risks identified on the prioritized risk response report are important enough to warrant a response.		6	
	H.4 Describe your approach for identifying the best response for each risk identified on the prioritized risk response report.		5	
	H.5 Describe your approach for determining which risk responses will provide the most overall security protection across all domains in the IT infrastructure.		5	
	H.6 Provide a narrative describing how to implement the selected risk responses for each domain in the IT infrastructure, including sequencing and cross-domain impact.		7	
	H.7 Describe your approach for preparing a formal risk response report that explains each of the selected responses to security risks across the seven domains of a typical IT infrastructure and the		7	

	recommended responses to each risk.			
		Total Raw Weighted Score: *(sum of Raw Weighted Scores above)*		

Total Raw Weighted Score ―――――――――――――――――――― **maximum possible raw weighted score** *(i.e., 5 x the sum of item weights above)*	**X40** *(maximum section score)*	**= SCORE:**	

TECHNICAL PROPOSAL & EVALUATION GUIDE — SECTION I

PROPOSER NAME:	

SECTION I — BIA, BCP, and DRP

The Proposer must address ALL BIA, BCP, and DRP section items and provide, in sequence, the information and documentation as required (referenced with the associated item references). A Proposal Evaluation Team, made up of three or more State employees, will independently evaluate and score the proposal's response to each item. Each evaluator will use the following whole number, raw point scale for scoring each item:

0 = little value	1 = poor	2 = fair	3 = satisfactory	4 = good	5 = excellent

The RFP Coordinator will multiply each item score by the assigned weight with the product being the item's raw weighted score for purposes of calculating the section score as detailed at the end of this table.

Any contract resulting from this RFP process shall incorporate by reference the respective proposal responses to all items below as a part of said contract (refer to *pro forma* contract "Special Terms and Conditions").

Proposal Page # (to be completed by Proposer)	Technical Approach Items	State Use ONLY		
		Score	Item Weight	Raw Weighted Score
	I.1 Provide a narrative describing your approach for ensuring operational continuity.		4	
	I.2 Describe your approach for identifying applications and functions that are critical to the operation of the organization.		4	
	I.3 Describe how you will conduct a formal Business Impact Analysis (BIA) to identify business-critical applications and functions.		4	
	I.4 Provide a narrative for how you will use the BIA to identify the resources necessary to ensure operational continuity.		4	
	I.5 Provide a narrative describing how you will use the BIA and identified critical resource list to develop a Business Continuity Plan (BCP).		5	
	I.6 Describe your approach for determining the cost and resources necessary to prepare for, and carry out, the BCP.		5	
	I.7 Provide a narrative describing how you will use the BIA, BCP, and identified critical resource list to develop a Disaster Recovery Plan (DRP).		5	
	I.8 Describe your approach for determining the cost and resources necessary to prepare for, and carry out, the DRP.		4	

| | **I.9** Describe your approach for testing the BCP and DRP to ensure they are effective and appropriate to protect operational continuity in the face of various interruptions. | | 5 | |

| **Total Raw Weighted Score:** *(sum of Raw Weighted Scores above)* |

| **Total Raw Weighted Score**
 ———————————————————
 maximum possible raw weighted score
 (i.e., 5 x the sum of item weights above) | **X40**
 (maximum section score) | **= SCORE:** | |

TECHNICAL PROPOSAL & EVALUATION GUIDE — SECTION J

PROPOSER NAME:	

SECTION J — LAYERED SECURITY SOLUTION

The Proposer must address ALL Layered Security Solution section items and provide, in sequence, the information and documentation as required (referenced with the associated item references). A Proposal Evaluation Team, made up of three or more State employees, will independently evaluate and score the proposal's response to each item. Each evaluator will use the following whole number, raw point scale for scoring each item:

0 = little value	*1 = poor*	*2 = fair*	*3 = satisfactory*	*4 = good*	*5 = excellent*

The RFP Coordinator will multiply each item score by the assigned weight with the product being the item's raw weighted score for purposes of calculating the section score as detailed at the end of this table.

Any contract resulting from this RFP process shall incorporate by reference the respective proposal responses to all items below as a part of said contract (refer to *pro forma* contract "Special Terms and Conditions").

Proposal Page # (to be completed by Proposer)	Technical Approach Items	State Use ONLY		
		Score	Item Weight	Raw Weighted Score
	J.1 Provide a narrative describing your approach for implementing a layered security solution to provide protection for critical resources and data.		4	
	J.2 Describe your approach for identifying the most sensitive resources and data that require specific protection from attack or failure.		4	
	J.3 Describe your approach for ensuring multiple controls to protect each identified resource or data collection to satisfy mandated security requirements.		4	
	J.4 Provide a narrative for how you will determine the most likely attack paths for each sensitive resource or data collection.		4	
	J.5 Provide a narrative describing how you will determine where to place controls across the seven domains of the typical IT infrastructure to provide multiple layers of security protection.		5	
	J.6 Describe your approach for ensuring that each sensitive resource or data collection is protected by multiple controls so that any control failure or compromise does not expose the protected resource or data collection.		5	
	J.7 Provide a narrative describing how the State can evaluate the effectiveness of each control in the layered security solution.		5	

	J.8 Describe your approach to documenting each layer of security controls, including the justification of each control, degree of protection, and ROI for the control and each logical control layer, as determined by its location in the typical IT infrastructure.		4	
	J.9 Provide a narrative describing how you will assess the layered security solution to ensure it maintains its design ROI and provides the desired level of protection.		5	

Total Raw Weighted Score:
(sum of Raw Weighted Scores above)

$$\frac{\textbf{Total Raw Weighted Score}}{\substack{\textbf{maximum possible raw weighted score} \\ \textit{(i.e., 5 x the sum of item weights above)}}} \quad \substack{\textbf{X40} \\ \textit{(maximum section score)}} \quad \textbf{= SCORE:}$$

COST PROPOSAL & SCORING GUIDE

NOTICE TO PROPOSER: This Cost Proposal MUST be completed EXACTLY as required.

PROPOSER NAME:	
SIGNATURE & DATE:	

NOTE: The signatory must be an individual or a company officer empowered to contractually bind the Proposer. If the Signatory is not the Proposer's chief executive or president, this Cost Proposal & Scoring Guide SHALL attach evidence showing the Signatory's authority to bind the Proposer.

COST PROPOSAL SCHEDULE

The proposed cost, detailed below, shall indicate the proposed price for providing the entire scope of service including all services as defined in the RFP Attachment 6.1, *Pro Forma* Contract Scope of Services for the total contract period. The proposed cost and the submitted technical proposal associated with this cost shall remain valid for at least 120 days subsequent to the date of the Cost Proposal opening and thereafter in accordance with any resulting contract between the Proposer and the State. All monetary amounts are United States currency.

The proposed hourly rates must be fully loaded to include all administrative, software tool, and travel costs.

The Proposer must enter only one rate per cost cell; the Proposer must **NOT** enter more than one rate or a range of rates in a single cost cell. The Proposer must **NOT** add any other information to the Cost Proposal.

The Proposer may enter zero (0) in a required proposed cost cell; however, the Proposer should not leave any proposed cost cell blank. For evaluation and contractual purposes, the State shall interpret a blank Proposed Cost cell as zero (0).

Cost Item Description	Proposed Hourly Rate			State Use ONLY		
	07/02/20xx - 07/01/20xx	07/02/20yy- 07/01/20yy	07/02/20zz- 07/01/20zz	Sum	Weight	Weighted Cost
Consultant With Greater Than 15 Years Information Security-Related Experience	$[HOURLY RATE]	$[HOURLY RATE]	$[HOURLY RATE]		625	
Consultant With 10 Years to 15 Years Information Security-Related Experience	$[HOURLY RATE]	$[HOURLY RATE]	$[HOURLY RATE]		625	
Consultant With 5 Years to Less Than 10 Years Information Security -Related Experience	$[HOURLY RATE]	$[HOURLY RATE]	$[HOURLY RATE]		625	
Consultant With Less Than 5 Years Information Security-Related Experience	$[HOURLY RATE]	$[HOURLY RATE]	$[HOURLY RATE]		625	

The RFP Coordinator shall use the evaluation cost amount derived from the proposed cost amounts above and the following formula to calculate the COST PROPOSAL SCORE. Calculations shall result in numbers rounded to two decimal places.	⬇
Evaluation Cost Amount: *(sum of all weighted cost amounts above)*	

Lowest Evaluation Cost Amount from <u>all</u> Proposals	**X 30**	**= SCORE:**	
―――――――――――――――――――――――	*(maximum section score)*		
Evaluation Cost Amount being evaluated			

PROPOSAL SCORE SUMMARY MATRIX

RFP Coordinator			Date			

QUALIFICATIONS & EXPERIENCE Maximum Points: 30	PROPOSER NAME		PROPOSER NAME		PROPOSER NAME	
EVALUATOR NAME						
EVALUATOR NAME						
EVALUATOR NAME						
EVALUATOR NAME						
REPEAT AS NECESSARY						
	AVERAGE SCORE:		AVERAGE SCORE:		AVERAGE SCORE:	
TECHNICAL APPROACH Maximum Points: 40						
EVALUATOR NAME						
EVALUATOR NAME						
EVALUATOR NAME						
EVALUATOR NAME						
REPEAT AS NECESSARY						
	AVERAGE SCORE:		AVERAGE SCORE:		AVERAGE SCORE:	
COST PROPOSAL Maximum Points: 30	SCORE:		SCORE:		SCORE:	
PROPOSAL SCORE Maximum Points: 100	TOTAL SCORE:		TOTAL SCORE:		TOTAL SCORE:	

ATTACHMENT 6.6

STATE GOVERNMENT
Information Security Assessment Services RFP
RFP #427.04-107-08
REFERENCE INFORMATION QUESTIONNAIRE

Proposer's Name: _____

Reference (Client Organization) Name:

_____

Person Responding to this Request for
Reference Information:
_____
Printed Name

_____
Signature **(MUST BE THE SAME AS THE SIGNATURE**
ACROSS THE ENVELOPE SEAL)

Person's Title: _____

Date Reference Form Was Completed: _____

NOTE: Reference should complete responses to the seven items that appear on the following pages. If completed using a Word document, use as much space as required. If completed manually, record response in space provided.

1. Describe the services provided by the vendor to your organization.

2. Please rate your overall satisfaction with the vendor on a scale of 1 to 5, with 1 being "least satisfied" and 5 being "most satisfied."

3. If you answered 3 or less to the previous question, what could the vendor have done to improve the rating?

4. Please indicate your level of satisfaction with the Proposer's project management structures, processes, and personnel. Use a scale of 1 to 5; with 1 being "least satisfied," and 5 being "most satisfied."

5. Rate your level of satisfaction with the vendor's line-level staff (e.g., business and systems analysts). Use a scale of 1 to 5; with 1 being "least satisfied" and 5 being "most satisfied."

6. As far as you know, has the vendor remained (or did the vendor remain) in compliance with the contract throughout their provision of services to your organization? If not, please explain.

7. Would you use the services of the vendor again? Indicate on a scale of 1 to 5: with 1 being "absolutely not" and 5 being "absolutely yes."

Template 6.7.1 – IT Security Policy Framework/RFP requirements

Instructions: Review the RFP IT Security Framework Requirements. For each identified requirement, find the corresponding controls that address it in the client's current environment. Note any requirements that have no existing controls.

RFP Requirement	Existing control(s)

Template 6.7.2 – Security Gap Analysis Recommendations

Instructions: Review the list of identified IT security gaps. For each identified security gap, list one or more recommended mitigation actions. Note any recommendations that span multiple domains in the IT infrastructure.

Identified gap (RFP requirement)	Mitigation recommendation	Domain (IT infrastructure)

Template 6.7.3 – Privacy Data Security Gaps

Instructions: Review the RFP's description of the client's current IT security policy framework, privacy data legal requirements, and the security gap analysis from the previous unit. Identify each of the security gaps that relate to protecting privacy data and describe each gap.

Provide a narrative explaining the exposure each privacy data gap represents to the client's organization and why it is important that the client mitigates it.

Privacy Data Security Gap	Exposure explanation	Mitigation importance

Template 6.7.4 – Privacy Data Security Gap Mitigation Recommendations

Instructions: Given an RFP, the results of an IT security compliance and governance gap analysis, and a list of privacy-data related gaps, describe each recommendation from the gap analysis and suggest at least one control change to satisfy the recommendation. Your report should address each point in the RFP technical description that relates to privacy data.

Provide a narrative explaining how each recommendation will satisfy a specific RFP requirement.

Privacy Data Security Gap	Mitigation control	Addresses RFP Requirement

Template 6.7.5 – Qualitative Risk Assessment Procedure

Instructions: Given an RFP and a security analysis project plan, prepare a procedure to conduct a security assessment for the Workstation and System/Applications domains in the client's IT infrastructure. Provide sufficient details that would enable a person in a position of responsibility in each area to conduct a security assessment by following the steps in the procedure (it is not necessary to provide low level details that would enable an untrained person to follow the steps in the procedure). Your procedure should address the major areas of concern in each domain.

Each procedure step should include the following information:

      Procedure step – A brief description of the step
      Explanation – A narrative describing the step and its purpose
      Action – A narrative describing the action needed to carry out this step

Procedure step	Explanation	Action

Template 6.7.6 – Qualitative Risk Analysis Procedure

Instructions: Using your qualitative risk analysis project plan, align the tasks and deliverables for risk assessment, analysis, and remediation with specific recommendations for addressing the risk elements. Include a cost proposal for identifying the tasks, deliverables, and man-hours required to perform the identified tasks.

Each procedure step should include the following information:
  Procedure step – A brief description of the step
  Explanation – A narrative describing the step and its purpose
  Action – A narrative describing the action needed to carry out this step

Procedure step	Explanation	Action

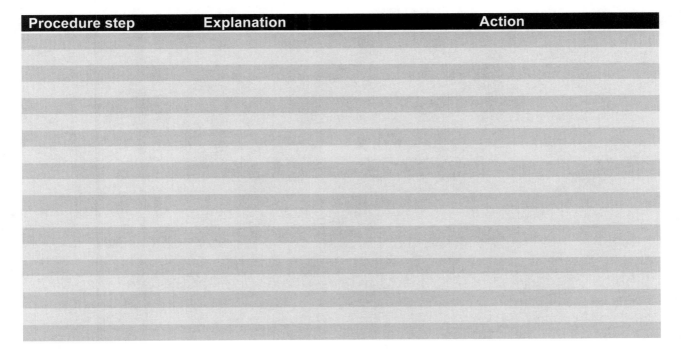

Template 6.7.7 – Mitigate Risks Procedure

Instructions: Using your prioritized risk mitigation project plan, align the tasks and deliverables for risk prioritization and remediation with specific recommendations for addressing the high-priority risk elements. Include a cost proposal for identifying the tasks, deliverables and man-hours required to perform the identified tasks.

Each procedure step should include the following information:
Procedure step – A brief description of the step
Explanation – A narrative describing the step and its purpose
Action – A narrative describing the action needed to carry out this step

Procedure step	Explanation	Action

Template 6.7.8 – Business Continuity Plan (BCP) Outline

Instructions: Upon review of the RFP technical description and output from a BIA, develop a BCP outline to address each mission critical application identified in the BIA. The BCP should list each mission critical application or function, the resources required to operate normally, and actions to minimize or recover from various types of interruptions.

Use the table to provide the following information (you may add lines as necessary):
    Item – A brief description of the items in the outline
    Details – Detailed description of this item
    Resources – Resources required to carry out each component of the plan

Item	Details	Resources
I. Purpose Statement	(provide a high level statement of purpose)	
II. Scope	(to whom do these procedures apply?)	
III. Assumptions	(assumptions on which the plan is based)	
IV. Critical business functions	(identified critical business functions)	
V. Risks to operation	(identified risks to critical business functions)	
VI. Strategies to address risks	(strategies to address each risk)	

Template 6.7.9 – Disaster Recovery Plan (DRP) Outline and Table of Contents

Instructions: Using the output from the BIA, create a DRP outline and table of contents. Then, use the BCP and DRP outline and table of contents to prepare a cost and resource estimate of the requirements to create the BCP and DRP. The estimates should include a cost proposal for identifying the tasks, deliverables, and man-hours required to perform the identified tasks.

Use the table to provide the following information (you may add lines as necessary):

Item – A brief description of the items in the outline
Details – Detailed description of this item
Cost – Estimated cost of this item
Man-hours – Estimated man-hours of this item

Item	Details	Cost	Man-hours
I. Purpose Statement	(provide a high level statement of purpose)		
II. Scope	(to whom do these procedures apply?)		
III. Assumptions	(assumptions on which the plan is based)		
IV. Update procedures	(procedures to update and amend the plan)		
V. DRP Normal Procedures	(normal procedures necessary to maintain readiness)		
VI. DRP Disaster Procedures	(procedures to follow after a disaster)		

Template 6.7.10 – Layered Security Solution Report

Instructions: Using your prioritized security control project plan, align the tasks and deliverables for security control prioritization with specific recommendations for implementing a multilayered security solution that spans all domains in a typical IT infrastructure. Prepare a report that provides the details of the actions carried out to implement the layered security solution plan. Include a cost proposal for identifying the tasks, deliverables, and man-hours required to perform the identified tasks. This report should contain details that explain each of the steps in the project plan.

Report Body (List each of the controls in your layered security solution. For each control, provide a brief description, the domain in which it resides, resources required, resources protected, and benefit expected.)

Control Identifier	Domain	Description	Required Resources	Resources Protected/Benefit

Template 6.7.11 – Layered Security Solution Executive Summary

Instructions: Using your prioritized security control project plan and layered security solution report, prepare an executive summary of the various layers of your security solution. Include high-level summaries for costs, deliverables, and man-hours required to perform the tasks identified in the layered security solution report.

Executive summary: Describe, in one page or less, how the security controls detailed in the body of the report will protect critical resources and data across the seven domains in the typical IT infrastructure.

_____

_____

_____

_____

_____

_____

_____

_____

_____

_____

_____

_____

_____

_____

_____

_____

STATE GOVERNMENT

Network Access Rights and Obligations
User Agreement Acknowledgement

As a user of State Government data and resources, I agree to abide by the Acceptable Use Network Access Rights and Obligations Policy and the following promises and guidelines as they relate to the policy established:

1. I will protect State confidential data, facilities and systems against unauthorized disclosure and/or use.

2. I will maintain all computer access codes in the strictest of confidence; immediately change them if I suspect their secrecy has been compromised, and will report activity that is contrary to the provisions of this agreement to my supervisor or a State-authorized Security Administrator.

3. I will be accountable for all transactions performed using my computer access codes.

4. I will not disclose any confidential information other than to persons authorized to access such information as identified by my section supervisor.

5. I agree to report to the Office for Information Resources (OIR) any suspicious network activity or security breach.

Privacy Expectations

The State Government actively monitors network services and resources, including, but not limited to, real time monitoring. Users should have no expectation of privacy. These communications are considered to be State property and may be examined by management for any reason including, but not limited to, security and/or employee conduct.

I acknowledge that I must adhere to this policy as a condition for receiving access to State Government data and resources.

I understand the willful violation or disregard of any of these guidelines, statute or policies may result in my loss of access and disciplinary action, up to and including termination of my employment, termination of my business relationship with the State Government, and any other appropriate legal action, including possible prosecution under the provisions of the Computer Crimes Act as cited by State Governing laws, mandates, and other applicable laws.

I have read and agree to comply with the policy set forth herein.

_____   _____
Type or Print Name   Last 4 digits of Social Security Number

_____   _____
Signature   Date

State Government

IT Infrastructure & Architecture

Overview of 7-Domains of a Typical IT Infrastructure & Architecture

The State Government IT Infrastructure for the purpose of our IS427 Capstone Course is to utilize the ISS Mock IT Infrastructure as the representative IT infrastructure. This is the same IT infrastructure used in the IS316 Network Security and IS317 Hacking Techniques course. This IT infrastructure includes the following elements as depicted in the 7-domains of a typical IT infrastructure:

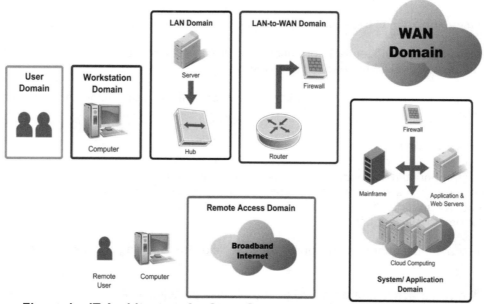

Figure 1 – IT Architecture for State Government Security Assessment

> **User Domain** – what risk does an organization have with its users and employees? What can help mitigate risk within this domain?

> **Workstation Domain** – what risk does an organization have regarding its physical workstation and hard drive, workstation OS, applications, software patching, and user's direct access to the Internet?

> **LAN Domain** – what risk does an organization have regarding file server OS, applications, software patching and user's direct access to data?

> **LAN-to-WAN Domain** – what risk does an organization have regarding unauthorized access, malicious software or code, and loss of data due to remote attacks from the Internet?

➤ **WAN Domain** – what risk does an organization have if the WAN circuits or connections are down?

➤ **Remote Access Domain** – what risk does an organization have regarding unauthorized access, data leakage, or inability to remotely access the IT infrastructure?

➤ **Systems/Applications Domain** – what risk does an organization have regarding production server OS, applications, and software patching?

By aligning the overall RFP's security assessment within this architecture and framework, the State can identify what risk is greatest in each of the individual domains and assess what risk mitigation strategies to deploy. The ultimate goal and objective of this RPF for security assessment services is to identify those gaps and weaknesses in the State's current enterprise security framework. The State desires a complete, layered security strategy that maximizes existing resources and incorporates new solutions for identified gaps.

State Government IT Infrastructure Overview & Network Diagram

For the purposes of this State Government RFP for security assessment services, the following shall be used to represent the IT infrastructure for purposes of responding to this RFP document and defining the scope:

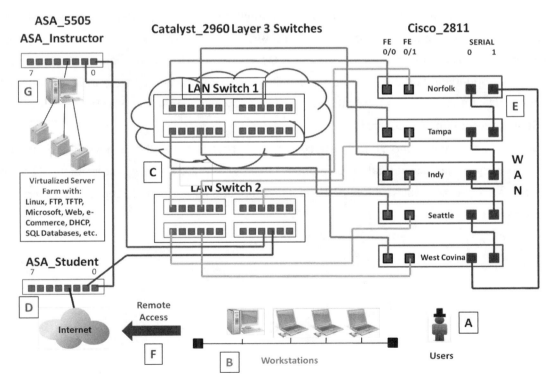

Figure 2 – State Government IT Infrastructure

In the above diagram, the following elements shall depict the State Government's IT Infrastructure:

A. **State Government End-Users** – these are the state government employees and authorized users of the State's IT infrastructure. Users must conform to the State's AUP, Right of Use Agreement, and Information Systems Security Policies

B. **Workstations** – these are the laptops, desktops, and mobile devices issued to State Government users. This is where the Workstation Domain resides and encompasses both the physical and logical configuration

C. **LAN Switches** – these are the LAN switches (layer 2 and layer 3) within the State Capital where the State's data center resides. This is where the LAN Domain resides and encompasses both the physical LAN and logical configuration. At the State's data center, use of VLANs and layer 2 and layer 3 switching is implemented

D. **DMZ** – ASA_Student mimics a demilitarized zone with 3 zones/VLANs configured on it. The DMZ acts as intermediate layer between the outside public Internet and the internal, closed State government network. This is where the LAN-to-WAN Domain resides and encompasses an IP stateful firewall, DMZ, and VPN termination for VPN tunnels from remote users requiring access to State government resources

E. **State Government Wide Area Network (WAN)** – this represents the State government WAN that connects and supports state government agency connectivity to other agencies and the State's data center. This is where the WAN Domain resides and encompasses the WAN service provider elements such as WAN circuit, IP router, firewalls, and managed services (if outsourced)

F. **Remote Access** – this represents the State Government's shared, broadband dedicated Internet access connection and the Remote Access Domain and encompasses the Internet connection and the IP router, firewalls, and other layered security solutions (i.e., VPN) for remote access to State government IT resources

G. **Server Farm** – this is the State's data center and represents the State's government agencies servers, applications, and data repositories. This is where the Systems/Applications Domain resides and encompasses the servers, cloud computing infrastructure, applications, and databases.

Statement of Work

For a State Government

Information Security Assessment (ISA)

1.0 INTRODUCTION

The State Government (the State) has an immediate requirement for contractual support for a review and assessment of its current Information Security Program. This review and assessment shall be defined in this statement of work (SoW). As a means of implementing the General Accounting Office's (GAO) five best practices for risk management, the State is undertaking a review of its entire Information Systems Security Program to include risk analysis/vulnerability assessment of its systems, assessment of the security program, security awareness training, development and enhancement of security plans, continuity and contingency planning (i.e., business impact analysis, business continuity, disaster recovery, incident response, etc.), and infrastructure protection review.

1.1 OBJECTIVE

This Statement of Work (SOW) is being issued on behalf of the State, located at State Government Tower, 100 1st Avenue, Capitol City, NY, U.S.A., 12345-1200.

The State is requesting qualified bidders to respond to this Request for Proposal (RFP) for Security Assessment services described in this SoW desired by the State Government.

1.2 BACKGROUND

1.2.1 Technical Infrastructure

The State's technical infrastructure is based on a hierarchical IP network infrastructure that supports agency to headquarters connectivity using a private class B 172.30.0.0/24 IP network addressing schema. Within the State's Capital is the State's data center and headquarters where 100Mbps and GigaBit Ethernet LANs and VLANs are deployed for segmented, department LAN traffic.

Server farms are connected behind security appliances support data center and headquarters connectivity to systems, applications, databases, and data.

Remote access from the public Internet is provided via a broadband, shared Internet access connection servicing all of State Government.

The State currently deploys a layered security solution of which a review and assessment of the current IT infrastructure's security deployment is required.

The State Government IT infrastructure is depicted below:

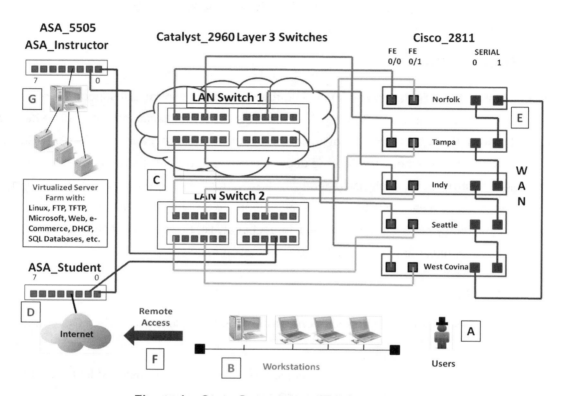

Figure 1 – State Government IT Infrastructure

In the above diagram, the following elements shall depict the State Government's IT Infrastructure:

A. **State Government End-Users** – these are the state government employees and authorized users of the State's IT infrastructure. Users must conform to the State's AUP, Right of Use Agreement, and Information Systems Security Policies

B. **Workstations** – these are the laptops, desktops, and mobile devices issued to State Government users. This is where the Workstation Domain resides and encompasses both the physical and logical configuration

C. **LAN Switches** – these are the LAN switches (layer 2 and layer 3) within the State Capital where the State's data center resides. This is where the LAN Domain resides and encompasses both the physical LAN and logical configuration. At the State's data center, use of VLANs and layer 2 and layer 3 switching is implemented

D. **DMZ** – ASA_Student mimics a demilitarized zone with 3 zones/VLANs configured on it. The DMZ acts as intermediate layer between the outside public Internet and the internal, closed State government network. This is where the LAN-to-WAN Domain resides and encompasses an IP stateful firewall, DMZ, and VPN termination for VPN tunnels from remote users requiring access to State government resources

E. **State Government Wide Area Network (WAN)** – this represents the State government WAN that connects and supports state government agency connectivity to other agencies and the State's data center. This is where the WAN Domain resides and encompasses the WAN service provider elements such as WAN circuit, IP router, firewalls, and managed services (if outsourced)

F. **Remote Access** – this represents the State Government's shared, broadband dedicated Internet access connection and the Remote Access Domain and encompasses the Internet connection and the IP router, firewalls, and other layered security solutions (i.e., VPN) for remote access to State government IT resources

G. **Server Farm** – this is the State's data center and represents the State's government agencies servers, applications, and data repositories. This is where the Systems/Applications Domain resides and encompasses the servers, cloud computing infrastructure, applications, and databases

1.2.2 IT Architecture

The State Government IT Architecture and security assessment will be aligned in accordance with the 7-domains of a typical IT infrastructure. By aligning the overall RFP's security assessment within this architecture and framework, the State can identify what risk is greatest in each of the individual domains and assess what risk mitigation strategies to deploy. The goal and objective of this RFP for security assessment services is to identify gaps and weaknesses in the State's current enterprise security framework. The State desires a complete, layered security strategy that maximizes existing resources and incorporates recommended solutions for identified gaps within the current Information Security Program implemented throughout the State.

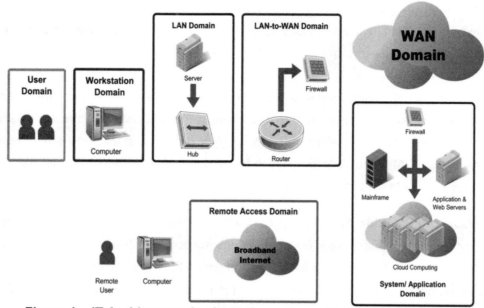

Figure 1 – IT Architecture for State Government Security Assessment

➢ **User Domain** – what risk does an organization have with its users and employees? What can help mitigate risk within this domain?

➢ **Workstation Domain** – what risk does an organization have regarding its physical workstation and hard drive, workstation OS, applications, software patching, and user's direct access to the Internet?

➢ **LAN Domain** – what risk does an organization have regarding file server OS, applications, software patching and user's direct access to data?

➢ **LAN-to-WAN Domain** – what risk does an organization have regarding unauthorized access, malicious software or code, and loss of data due to remote attacks from the Internet?

➢ **WAN Domain** – what risk does an organization have if the WAN circuits or connections are down?

➢ **Remote Access Domain** – what risk does an organization have regarding unauthorized access, data leakage, or inability to remotely access the IT infrastructure?

➢ **Systems/Applications Domain** – what risk does an organization have regarding production server OS, applications, and software patching?

2.0 SCOPE

The State has an immediate requirement for contractual support for technical security consulting services for its Information Security Program. The State is undertaking a review of its entire Systems Security Program to include risk analysis/vulnerability assessment of its systems, assessment of the automated security program, security awareness training, development and enhancement of security plans, continuity and contingency planning, and infrastructure protection review.

The first phase of this project consists of a risk analysis/vulnerability assessment of specified State systems, primarily the State Government IT Infrastructure aligned to the IT Architecture consisting of the seven domains of a typical IT infrastructure. For those systems that contain or process privacy information, further risk assessment to ensure privacy protection will be conducted as part of a later task.

The second phase of this project consists of an assessment and recommendations for the State's information security program and specific enhancements in the area of security awareness and training. Security plans for selected State systems will be reviewed and updated as part of this assessment phase. Specific tasks for the project are described below.

The State requires contractors with technical expertise in the development and assessment of information security programs, development of security plans, experience in conducting risk analyses and vulnerability assessments, expertise in continuity and contingency planning, and proficiency in the development of security awareness training programs.

3.0   TASKS

3.1   Task #1. General Description

The Contractor will conduct a security gap analysis, risk analysis and vulnerability assessment for State systems. The systems to be reviewed will be the State's database and web server computers.

3.1.1   Task #1. Responsibilities

The contractor, working with the State's computer security program manager and with other security officials responsible for the respective State systems must conduct a complete security gap analysis and risk analysis. The security gap analysis will consist of organizing a comprehensive list of all known risks, threats, and vulnerabilities and current security controls and countermeasures implemented that do or do not fulfill one or more policy statements or regulatory requirements. The risk analysis for each system will be performed following the State's IT Architecture framework consisting of the seven domains of a typical IT infrastructure. Within each of these domains, the following shall be the approach/methodology for performing the gap analysis and security assessment:

> Definition of scope of analysis

> Identification of the State's critical assets

> Determination of the best analytical (qualitative/quantitative) base for an evaluation

> Identification of potential risks, threats, and vulnerabilities

> Evaluation of the risk profile (risk, threat, & vulnerability assessment)

> Risk remediation recommendations: short-term and long-term with cost-magnitude estimates

The process for the review and creation of the gap analysis and risk analysis report will be the same for each system and domain under review. The deliverables identified below are required for each system and domain where the gap analysis and security assessment is to focus.

3.1.2   Task #1. Deliverables

1.   **Draft outline.** A written draft outline of the security gap analysis and risk analysis reports must be provided. These outlines will provide the basis for the draft and final report deliverables for this task. The outline must contain sufficient detail to indicate all pertinent areas of the analysis will be addressed and should include all areas in which gaps will be identified and risks will be

reviewed, e.g., physical, operating system, application, data, emergency preparedness, backup, disaster recovery, etc. This deliverable will be required for ONLY the first security gap analysis and risk analysis. All subsequent security gap analyses and risk analyses will utilize the same format. This deliverables are due 5 working days after the start of this task. The government will provide written comments within 5 working days after receipt of the draft outlines.

2. **Draft report.** A written draft report, based on the approved draft outline, which contains approximately the first 50% of the elements required in each of the reports is required as a deliverable. The draft report must contain the complete write-ups for the first half of the security gap analysis and risk analysis, including but not limited to the first 3 items noted above, as well as the assessment of physical, data, and operating system security. This deliverable is due 20 working days after the government's acceptance of the draft outline. The government will have 10 working days to review the deliverable and provide written comments to the contractor.

3. **Final report.** The final report must address all written government comments on the prior draft. The final report must include the complete security gap analysis and risk analysis for the system, which includes all items identified in the draft report, the remainder of the risk identification section, and the final 3 items noted above. This final report deliverable is due 20 working days from the receipt of the government's comments on the draft report. The government will have 10 working days to review the final report and provide written comments to the contractor. The contractor must incorporate or address all of the government's written comments before the deliverable will be accepted as final by the government. The final deliverable is due 5 days after receipt of the government's written comments.

3.2   Task #2. General Description

The State requires a detailed review and assessment of the State's Information Security Program relative to state laws and guidance and other State agencies' best practices.

3.2.1   Task #2. Responsibilities

The Contractor will review State's existing information security program as documented in the current and proposed draft revision of the State's Information Security Policies & Framework.

The review will identify any deficiencies or weaknesses in the State's Information Security Program. In addition, the review will evaluate other State Government agencies whom have existing information systems security programs that could serve as models of "best practices" for the entire State. The deliverables from the prior task (security gap analysis and risk assessment) will also be included in the review.

The review will include specific recommendations to correct any deficiencies or weaknesses and improve the State Security Program relative to "best practices" that are applicable to the State. The recommendations must be specific and contain sufficient detail to be capable of being implemented. The recommendations must also include the level of effort and/or cost required to complete each separate recommendation as part of the vendor/consultant's deliverables.

3.2.2 Task #2. Deliverables

1. **Report outline.** A written report outline which identifies specific areas required and best practices to be assessed in the review of the State Security Program must be developed. This outline will provide the basis for the draft and final report deliverable for this task. The outline must contain sufficient detail to indicate all relative Federal statutory requirements have been addressed. This outline must be provided to the government in both hard-copy and electronic format 10 working days after the initial kick-off meeting for this task. The government will provide written comments on the report outline within 5 working days of receipt of the report outline.

2. **Draft report.** A written draft report, based on the approved draft matrix (outline) which contains the results of the review of the State Security Program relative to state statutory requirements and state agencies' "best practices" is required as a deliverable. The draft report must contain sufficient detail to indicate **all** relative. Weaknesses or deficiencies need to be expressly identified as such with the state law, guideline, or best practice clearly identified.

   The draft report need not contain the complete recommendation for correction/ enhancement of all of the identified weaknesses or deficiencies. For those items in which the recommendation has been written, the costs and resources required to implement the recommendation must be documented. This deliverable in both hard-copy and electronic format is due 20 working days after the start of this task. The government will provide written comments on the draft within 5 working days of receipt of the deliverable.

3. **Final report.** The final report must address all written government comments on the prior draft. The final report must include all weaknesses or deficiencies and the recommendations for correction of the weakness or deficiency. The recommendations must include the level of effort or cost required to correct the deficiency and must contain enough detail that the recommendation would be capable of being implemented. The report should also identify any areas of the State Security Directive which must be modified in light of these recommendations. The final report deliverable is due 15 working days from the receipt of the government's comments on the draft report. The government will have 10 working days to review the final report and provide written comments to the contractor. The contractor must incorporate or

address all of the government's written comments before the deliverable will be accepted as final by the government. The contractor will have 5 days to finalize the report.

3.3 Task #3. General Description

The State requires technical support in the area of Security Training and Security Awareness. The State requires the conducting of security training for the State's system owners. The State also requires the development of curriculum or security awareness documentation that can be used on an Agency-wide basis.

3.3.1 Task #3. Responsibilities

The contractor will develop security training materials specifically designed to assist key security staff and State officials responsible for major application and general support systems to participate in the enhancement or development of the security plans for their systems. The objectives of this training will be to orient the staff and appropriate officials concerning their security role and responsibilities relative to their system and to orient them for their role in assisting the Contractor with the task of developing security plans and operational procedures (described below). The training modules should be developed following the general outline documented in NIST Special Publication 800-18, "Guide for Developing Security Plans for Information Technology Systems". The training should be considered fairly high-level and is expected to consist of approximately 6-8 classroom hours of training material.

The contractor will also conduct an assessment of the current security information provided to all State employees relative to that required by current government-wide directives. Based upon this assessment, the contractor will update/develop, in conjunction with State requirements as identified in the risk analysis task (defined above), a security awareness brochure/pamphlet or recommend commercial-off-the-shelf training materials that can be provided/used by all State personnel. This brochure will contain information required by government-wide directives and specific State implementing procedures and be designed to provide to all employees their individual security responsibilities.

3.3.2 Task #3. Deliverables

1. **Draft outline of security training course.** A draft outline of the security training curriculum must be provided. The outline must be segmented in modules, contain a description of the objective of each module, and an estimated length of time to cover the module. This deliverable is due 5 working days after the completion of Task #1. The government will have 3 working days to complete their review and provide written comments to the contractor.

2. **Security Training Course materials.** The entire course must be delivered as a completed package. All modules must be completely defined with appropriate objectives of each module

identified. The materials should be sufficiently documented so that they can be used as a reference guide in the development of the key components in a security plan. This deliverable is due 15 working days after the completion of the prior deliverable in this task (draft outline). The deliverable must be submitted in a bound hard-copy (two copies) and electronic format. The course materials will become the property of the State. The government will have 10 working days to review the course materials and provide written comments to the contractor. The contractor will have 5 working days to incorporate and/or address all of the comments provided by the government.

3. **Security Training Class.** The contractor must conduct the security training class based on the approved course materials. The class will be approximately 6-8 hours in length and be targeted to the system owners of the key systems identified in the risk assessment. The class will be conducted in the State's headquarters training facility. The State will be responsible for the replication of the materials for the training class.

4. **Employee Security Awareness Training.** The contractor must provide either written employee security awareness training materials both hard copy and electronic format or recommendations on products which would meet the State requirements. This deliverable is due 10 working days after the completion of the Security Training Class. The government will have five working days to review the information and provide written comments to the contractor. The contractor will have five working days to incorporate and/or address all comments provided by the government.

3.4   Task #4. General Description

The Contractor will review existing computer security plans and operational procedures for State's major application and general support systems written to comply with all current legislation and regulations, and will revise or update the plans to reflect system changes. For those major applications or general support systems for which no computer security plan exists, the Contractor will create new plans.

3.4.1 Task #4. Responsibilities

The contractor, working with State's computer security program manager and with other security officials responsible for the respective State systems will update or create new security plans. The revised and new plans will be concise, but will be written to conform to NIST Special Publication 800-18 (Guide for Developing Security Plans for Information Technology Systems). The security plan for each system will

94

clearly define the security requirements, describe the controls in place or plan to meet these requirements, and delineate the responsibilities and expected behavior of all individuals who access the system.

The State has a number of systems which require review and/or development of security plans. The actual number of systems for which security plans will be completed will depend on project funding.

The process for the review and creation of the security plans will be the same for each system under review. The deliverables identified below are required for each system. The complete set of deliverables will be received and accepted prior to the start of the process for the subsequent system's security plan.

3.4.2 Task #4. Deliverables

1. **Draft outline.** A written draft outline of the security plan must be provided. This outline will provide the basis for the draft and final report deliverable for this task. The outline must contain sufficient detail to indicate all pertinent areas of the security plan will be addressed. It must also include, at a minimum, its categorization as either major application or general support system, identification regarding who is responsible for the system, the purpose of the system and the sensitivity level of the system. This outline must be provided to the government in both hard-copy and electronic format 5 working days after the initial kick-off meeting for each system having a security plan developed/updated. The government will provide written comments on the draft outline within 5 working days of receipt of this draft deliverable.

2. **Draft report.** A written draft report, based on the approved draft outline, which contains all of the elements required in the security plan will be required as a deliverable. The draft report must contain all elements of the security plan including, but not limited to, system identification, system name/title, responsible organization, information contact, assignment of security responsibility, system operational status, general description, system environment, system interconnection/information sharing, sensitivity of information handled, management controls, and operational controls. As a draft, the elements in each section can be identified in bullet format, i.e., the complete write-up does not need to be drafted, but must contain enough information to identify key points for each section. If specific items were unable to be identified, e.g., management or operational controls, these items must be clearly identified and a recommendation for corrective action be made. Any such recommendation should be identified

and documented as separate from the actual security plan. This deliverable is due 20 working days after the government's acceptance of the draft outline. The government will have 10 working days to review the deliverable and provide written comments to the contractor.

3. **Final report.** The final report must address all written government comments on the prior draft. The final report must include the complete security plan for the system. All items identified in the draft report in bullet format must be expanded into a complete write-up. If specific items were unable to be identified, e.g., operational or management controls, these items must be clearly identified and a recommendation for corrective action be made. Any such recommendation should be identified and documented as separate from the actual security plan. This final report deliverable is due 20 working days from the receipt of the government's comments on the draft report. The government will have 10 working days to review the final report and provide written comments to the contractor. The contractor must incorporate or address all of the government's written comments before the deliverable will be accepted as final by the government. The final deliverable is due 5 days after receipt of the government's written comments.

3.5   Task #5. General Description

The Contractor will review existing processes supported by computer software or IT resources. The Contractor will assess the impact of interruption of any critical processes and develop plans to address interruptions of any type. For those major applications or general support systems for which no interruption plan exists, the Contractor will create new plans.

3.5.1   Task #5. Responsibilities

The contractor, working with State's computer security program manager and with other security officials responsible for the respective State systems will update or create new critical process interruption plans, including a formal Business Continuity Plan (BCP) and Disaster Recovery Plan (DRP). The BCP and DRP for each system will clearly define the continuity requirements, describe the controls in place or plan to meet these requirements, and delineate the responsibilities and expected behavior of all individuals who participate in ensuring operational continuity.

The State has a number of systems that support critical processes and require review and/or development of continuity plans. The actual number of systems for which continuity plans will be completed will depend on project funding.

The process for the review and creation of the continuity plans will be the same for each system under review. The deliverables identified below are required for each system. The complete set of deliverables will be received and accepted prior to the start of the process for the subsequent system's security plan.

3.5.2 Task #5. Deliverables

1. **Draft outline.** A written draft outline of the continuity and disaster response plan must be provided. This outline will provide the basis for the draft and final report deliverable for this task. The outline must contain sufficient detail to indicate all pertinent areas of the continuity and disaster response plan will be addressed. It must also include, at a minimum, its categorization as either major application or general support system, identification regarding who is responsible for the system, the purpose of the system and the sensitivity level of the system. This outline must be provided to the government in both hard-copy and electronic format 5 working days after the initial kick-off meeting for each system having a security plan developed/updated. The government will provide written comments on the draft outline within 5 working days of receipt of this draft deliverable.

2. **Draft report.** A written draft report, based on the approved draft outline, which contains all of the elements required in the continuity and disaster response plan will be required as a deliverable. The draft report must contain all elements of the continuity and disaster response plan including, but not limited to, system identification, system name/title, responsible organization, information contact, assignment of continuity and disaster response responsibility, system operational status, general description, system environment, system interconnection/information sharing, sensitivity of information handled, management controls, and operational controls. As a draft, the elements in each section can be identified in bullet format, i.e., the complete write-up does not need to be drafted, but must contain enough information to identify key points for each section. If specific items were unable to be identified, e.g., management or operational controls, these items must be clearly identified and a recommendation for corrective action be made. Any such recommendation should be identified and documented as separate from the actual security plan. This deliverable is due 20 working days after the government's acceptance of the draft outline. The government will have 10 working days to review the deliverable and provide written comments to the contractor.

3. **Final report.** The final report must address all written government comments on the prior draft. The final report must include the complete continuity and disaster response plan for the system. All items identified in the draft report in bullet format must be expanded into a complete write-up. If specific items were unable to be identified, e.g., operational or management controls, these items must be clearly identified and a recommendation for corrective action be made. Any such

recommendation should be identified and documented as separate from the actual security plan. This final report deliverable is due 20 working days from the receipt of the government's comments on the draft report. The government will have 10 working days to review the final report and provide written comments to the contractor. The contractor must incorporate or address all of the government's written comments before the deliverable will be accepted as final by the government. The final deliverable is due 5 days after receipt of the government's written comments.

4.0   GOVERNMENT FURNISHED EQUIPMENT AND FACILITIES

4.1   Support Provided by the State

The State will provide the following facilities, tools, supplies, and resources to aid the contractor in the accomplishment of the tasks and functions described above.

1. The State will provide space (a desk and chair) at our headquarters site for up to two contractors for this project.

2. Each contractor will be provided with at least one (1) telephone and one (1) computer when working at the headquarters site. Telephones may only be used in accordance with Federal Guidelines and Standards to conduct State-related business and may not be used to conduct non-State contractor business.

3. On-site contractor personnel have the use of copiers located in the State headquarters building. Copying paper and acetate materials will be supplied by the Government as needed.

4. Contractor personnel will be issued building IDs to facilitate access to the headquarters building.

4.2   Support Not Provided by the State (Must be Supplied by the Contractor)

The following operational support will NOT be provided by the State as part of this contract. It is the responsibility of the contractor to supply these items, as needed, to accomplish the tasks described above.

1. Office supplies such as paper, pens, pencils, clips, staplers, or any other general office supplies.

2. Secretarial or clerical support.

3. Tools required to complete any of the tasks.

5.0 PERSONNEL

Resumes for all individuals proposed for each task should be submitted as part of the proposal in accordance with previous standards set under the State Technology Service's (STS) Safeguard contract. In addition, the specific staff categories described below must also be addressed. Personnel must have demonstrated experiences, documented in their resume, in support of the specific task for which they are being proposed.

1. Project management and hands-on experience in the performance and leadership of project teams in conducting security program reviews and assessments, development of security awareness programs, and review and development of security plans. Expertise should be demonstrated by showing a thorough knowledge of performing these services in the government sector following State and Federal guidelines. CCSP (Certified Computer Security Professional), CISSP (Certified Information Systems Security Professional), or CISA (Certified Information Systems Auditor) is highly desirable.

2. Security analyst skill set is required. Skills in the assessment and development of security plans, conducting of risk analyses and vulnerability assessments based upon the Federal sector requirements. Current experience in reviewing, documenting, and auditing security requirements for systems built using state-of-the-art technologies, e.g., Internet/Intranet services, WEB and WEB-enabled applications, HP UX, Oracle dbms, etc. Expertise in performing information systems auditing is required.

3. Security training expertise is required. Knowledge of security training materials, experience in developing security curriculum, classroom experience in training managers and IT technical specialists in specific security awareness and information security responsibilities must be demonstrated.

4. Expertise in electronic signature technologies, encryption techniques, and other state-of-the-art security technologies. Demonstrated experience in implementation of such security technologies in a WEB/Internet environment is highly desirable.

5. The specific individuals proposed for each task must be made available, at the appropriate time in the project, to work full-time on the tasks described in this Statement of Work.

6. All personnel with the above defined skill set related to this Statement of Work are considered Key Personnel. Offerors may NOT replace Key Personnel after the technical evaluation is completed unless the individual is no longer an employee of the Offeror or unless written permission is obtained from the State. This clause supersedes any other statements on personnel associated with this contract. A bid on this Statement of Work constitutes acceptance of this clause.

7. All personnel must be fully trained and ready for the tasks for which they are proposed, prior to becoming billable through this contract.

STATE GOVERNMENT

Acceptable Use Policy

Network Access Rights and Obligations

Purpose

To establish guidelines for State-owned hardware and software, computer network access and usage, Internet and email usage, telephony, and security and privacy for users of the State Government's IT Infrastructure and Wide Area Network.

References

State Government Blue Book – State Laws, Mandates, and Acts
State Government Security Policies

Objectives

- Ensure the protection of proprietary, personal, privileged, or otherwise sensitive data and resources that may be processed in any manner by the State, or any agent for the State.

- Provide uninterrupted network resources to users.

- Ensure proper usage of networked information, programs and facilities offered by the State Government networks.

- Maintain security of and access to networked data and resources on an authorized basis.

- Secure email from unauthorized access.

- Protect the confidentiality and integrity of files and programs from unauthorized users.

- Inform users there is no expectation of privacy in their use of State-owned hardware, software, or computer network access and usage.

- Provide Internet and email access to the users of the State Government networks.

Scope

This Acceptable Use Policy applies to all individuals who have been provided access rights to the State Government IT infrastructure and Wide Area Network. State provided email, and/or Internet via agency issued network or system User ID's. The scope does not include State phone systems, fax machines, copiers, State issued cell phones or pagers unless those services are delivered over the State's IP network.

Use and Prohibitions:

A. Network Resources

State employees, vendors/business partners/sub-recipients, local governments, and other governmental agencies may be authorized to access state network resources to perform business functions with or on behalf of the State. Users must be acting within the scope of their employment or contractual relationship with the State and must agree to abide by the terms of this agreement as evidenced by his/her signature. It is recognized that there may be incidental personal use of State Network Resources.

Employees should be aware that all usage may be monitored and that there is no right to privacy. Various transactions resulting from network usage are the property of the state and are thus subject to open records laws.

Prohibitions

- Sending or sharing with unauthorized persons any information that is confidential by law, rule or regulation.

- Installing software that has not been authorized by the Office for Information Resources of the Department of Finance and Administration.

- Attaching processing devices that have not been authorized by the Office for Information Resources of the Department of Finance and Administration.

- Using network resources to play or download games, music or videos that are not in support of business functions.

- Leaving workstation unattended without engaging password protection for the keyboard or workstation.

- Utilizing unauthorized peer-to-peer networking or peer-to-peer file sharing.

- Using network resources in support of unlawful activities as defined by federal, state, and local law.

- Utilizing network resources for activities that violate conduct policies established by the Department of Human Resources or the Agency where the user is employed or under contract.

B. Email

Email and calendar functions are provided to expedite and improve communications among network users.

Prohibitions

- Sending unsolicited junk email or chain letters (e.g. "spam") to any users of the network.

- Sending any material that contains viruses, Trojan horses, worms, time bombs, cancel bots, or any other harmful or deleterious programs.

- Sending copyrighted materials via email that is either not within the fair use guidelines or without prior permission from the author or publisher.

- Sending or receiving communications that violate conduct policies established by the Department of Human Resources or the Agency where the user is employed or under contract.

- Sending confidential material to an unauthorized recipient, or sending confidential e-mail without the proper security standards (including encryption if necessary) being met.

- Email created, sent or received in conjunction with the transaction of official business are public records in accordance with T.C.A 10-7-301 through 10-7-308, and the rules of the Public Records Commission. A public record is defined as follows:

  "Public record(s)" or "state record(s)" means all documents, papers, letters, maps, books, photographs, microfilms, electronic data processing files and output, films, sound recordings or other material, regardless of physical form or characteristics made or received pursuant to law or ordinance or in connection with the transaction of official business by any governmental agency.

State records are open to public inspection unless they are protected by State or Federal law, rule, or regulation. Because a court could interpret state records to include draft letters, working drafts of reports, and what are intended to be casual comments, be aware that anything sent as electronic mail could be made available to the public.

C. Internet Access

Internet access is provided to network users to assist them in performing the duties and responsibilities associated with their positions.

Prohibitions

- Using the Internet to access non-State provided web email services.

- Using Instant Messaging or Internet Relay Chat (IRC).

- Using the Internet for broadcast audio for non-business use.

- Utilizing unauthorized peer-to-peer networking or peer-to-peer file sharing.

- Using the Internet when it violates any federal, state or local law.

Statement of Consequences

Noncompliance with this policy may constitute a legal risk to the State, an organizational risk to the State in terms of potential harm to employees or citizen security, or a security risk to the State's Network Operations and the user community, and/or a potential personal liability. The presence of unauthorized data in the State network could lead to liability on the part of the State as well as the individuals responsible for obtaining it.

Statement of Enforcement

Noncompliance with this policy may result in the following immediate actions.

1. Written notification will be sent to the Agency Head and to designated points of contact in the User Agency's Human Resources and Information Technology Resource Offices to identify the user and the nature of the noncompliance as "cause". In the case of a vendor, subrecipient, or contractor, the contract administrator will be notified.

2. User access may be terminated immediately by the Systems Administrator, and the user may be subject to subsequent review and action as determined by the agency, department, board, or commission leadership, or contract administrator.

STATE GOVERNMENT

Acceptable Use Policy

Network Access Rights and Obligations

User Agreement Acknowledgement

As a user of State Government data and resources, I agree to abide by the Acceptable Use Network Access Rights and Obligations Policy and the following promises and guidelines as they relate to the policy established:

1. I will protect State confidential data, facilities and systems against unauthorized disclosure and/or use.

2. I will maintain all computer access codes in the strictest of confidence; immediately change them if I suspect their secrecy has been compromised, and will report activity that is contrary to the provisions of this agreement to my supervisor or a State-authorized Security Administrator.

3. I will be accountable for all transactions performed using my computer access codes.

4. I will not disclose any confidential information other than to persons authorized to access such information as identified by my section supervisor.

5. I agree to report to the Office for Information Resources (OIR) any suspicious network activity or security breach.

Privacy Expectations

The State Government actively monitors network services and resources, including, but not limited to, real time monitoring. Users should have no expectation of privacy. These communications are considered to be State property and may be examined by management for any reason including, but not limited to, security and/or employee conduct.

I acknowledge that I must adhere to this policy as a condition for receiving access to State Government data and resources.

I understand the willful violation or disregard of any of these guidelines, statute or policies may result in my loss of access and disciplinary action, up to and including termination of my employment, termination of my business relationship with the State Government, and any other appropriate legal action, including possible prosecution under the provisions of the Computer Crimes Act as cited at TCA 39-14-601 et seq., and other applicable laws.

I have read and agree to comply with the policy set forth herein.

_____   _____
Type or Print Name   Last 4 digits of Social Security Number

_____   _____
Signature   Date

STATE GOVERNMENT

OFFICE OF INFORMATION RESOURCES (OIR)

ENTERPRISE

DATA CLASSIFICATION STANDARD

v1.0

For Public Release

Classification	Minimum User Authentication Requirements	Minimum Transport Requirements	Minimum Storage Requirements
SECRET: This classification applies to data that is sensitive in nature that requires special precautions to prevent unauthorized viewing. Unauthorized disclosure of this data carries a CRITICAL threat definition. Disclosure of data in this category must be made by the data owner in accordance with defined policies defined by the data owner.	Two-factor	Data requires encryption during transport.	Electronic versions must be stored on network drives that are behind a firewall and stored encrypted. Backups must be secured in locked cabinets or physically secured areas. Paper versions must be stored in locked cabinets or physically secured areas and must be labeled as "SECRET".
CONFIDENTIAL: This data must be protected from disclosure by state or federal statute. Its unauthorized disclosure could seriously and adversely impact the State, its business partners, and/or its customers. Disclosure of data in this category must be made by the data owner in accordance with defined policies defined by the data owner.	Two levels unless published on the organization's Intranet, then only one is needed *	Data transported outside the intranet requires encryption during transport.	Electronic versions must be stored on network drives that are behind a firewall or stored encrypted. Backups must be secured in locked cabinets or physically secured areas. Paper versions must be stored in locked cabinets or physically secured areas and must be labeled as "CONFIDENTIAL".
INTERNAL USE: This classification applies to information that is intended for use within the organization. While data in this category is not protected by statute, its disclosure could adversely impact the organization, its business partners, and/or its customers. Disclosure of data in this category must be made by the data owner and in accordance with defined policies defined by the data owner.	Single level *	Encryption should be considered, depending on the sensitivity of the data and depending on the networks over which the data will be sent.	Electronic versions should be stored on network drives that are behind a firewall. If the data is stored on a notebook or workstation, encryption is not mandatory but should be considered. Paper versions do not have to be stored in locked cabinets or physically secured areas; however, care should be taken not to remove "INTERNAL USE" documents from the office and if they are, proper care must be taken by the user of the printed data.
PUBLIC: Data in this classification can be disclosed to any one for any reason without any negative impact to the organization, its business partners, and/or its customers.	None	None	There are no privacy requirements for electronic storage of data in this category. However, the impact of the denial of availability of data or of recovering lost or damaged data may necessitate levels of protection commensurate with the threats. Paper versions do not have to be stored in locked cabinets or physically secured areas.

STATE GOVERNMENT

OFFICE OF INFORMATION RESOURCES (OIR)

ENTERPRISE

INFORMATION SYSTEMS SECURITY POLICIES

V1.0

For Public Release

Table of Contents

1. EXECUTIVE SUMMARY

The main purpose of this document is to define the information systems security policies of the State Government along with the organization and framework/structure required to communicate, implement and support these policies. Information is an asset, which like any other asset owned by the State, has significant value to the stakeholders of the State. Information systems security is a critical component that is required to enable and ensure the availability, integrity and confidentiality of data, network and processing resources required for the State to perform its business and operational practices. This policy document has been developed to establish and uphold the minimum requirements that are necessary to protect information resources (assets) against unavailability, unauthorized or unintentional access, modification, destruction or disclosure as set forth by the State Government's Office of Information Resources.

The scope of this document is intended to cover any information asset owned, leased or controlled by the State and the methodologies and practices of external entities that require access to the State's information resources. This document seeks to protect:

All desktop computing systems, servers, data storage devices, communication systems, firewalls, routers, switches, hubs, personal digital assistants (PDAs) and mobile devices (computing platforms) owned by the State where lawfully permitted.

Any computing platforms, operating system software, middleware or application software under the control of third parties that connect in any way to the State enterprise computing or telecommunications network.

All data, information, knowledge, documents, presentations, databases or other information resource stored on the State's computing platforms and/or transferred by the State's enterprise network.

This document applies to all full- and part-time employees of the State and all third parties, contractors or vendors who work on State premises or remotely connect their computing platforms to the State's computing platforms.

By establishing the appropriate policy framework and utilizing a documented policy development process that includes all stakeholders, the State envisions maximum voluntary compliance. The policy development and implementation process includes an impact analysis, input from Agency IT professionals and approval by the Chief Information Security Officer (CISO) and executive management team within the Office for Information Resources, Department of Finance and Administration.

All information resources and any information system owned by the State shall be protected from unauthorized disclosure, use, modification or destruction in a manner commensurate with their value, sensitivity and criticality to the business and operation of the state government and those they serve. Access to information technology assets will be granted using the principle of least privilege.

All of the approved policies will support the requirements of the State Government's Information Systems Security Policy Framework. This policy framework is set for public release to be shared and distributed state-wide.

2. INTRODUCTION

The Information Security Challenge

Information technology (IT) solutions are driven by the demands of our daily business activities. The ability to procure efficient communication, IT resources and business processes at a low cost is a foundational component of successful IT programs. This integration moves quickly to align itself with the "just in time" requirements of the business. Given the growth demands of the business along with the associated time sensitive integration strategies, we are presented with new risks at every turn. Organizations will frequently take risks in order to meet those time sensitive business requirements, sometimes cutting out existing processes which could introduce delays, or bypassing process requirements all together to keep up with the demand of the customers whom they serve. This practice, also known as risk management, is a component of any successful business. Modern enterprises will implement risk management and/or information security programs to mitigate these risks.

The State has recognized the need and put the information security programs to work. One of the main goals of any successful information security program is to protect the organization's revenues, resources, and reputation. This is accomplished through several means. Some examples are implementing risk management methodologies, security architectures, control frameworks and security policy to list a few.

Security policy is a foundational component of any successful security program. The Enterprise Information Security Policies for the State Government are based on the International Standards Organization (ISO) 17799 standard framework. The policies are designed to comply with applicable laws and regulations; however, if there is a conflict, applicable laws and regulations will take precedence. The policies included in this document are to be considered the minimum requirements for providing a secure operational environment. These policies shall form the basis for the State's Enterprise Information Security Policies Framework.

Scope (2.1)

The scope of this document is intended to cover any information asset owned, leased or controlled by the State Government and the methodologies and practices of external entities that require access to the State Government's information resources. This document seeks to protect:

All desktop computing systems, servers, data storage devices, communication systems, firewalls, routers, switches, hubs, personal digital assistants (PDAs) and mobile devices (computing platforms) controlled by the State Government where lawfully permitted.

Any computing platforms, operating system software, middleware or application software under the control of the State Government, or by third parties, operated on behalf of the State Government that connect in any way to the State's enterprise computing or telecommunications network.

All data, information, knowledge, documents, presentations, databases or other information resource stored on the State Government's computing platforms and/or transferred by the State's enterprise network.

All full- and part-time employees of the State Government and all third parties, contractors, or vendors who work on State premises or remotely connect their computing platforms to the State Government's computing platforms shall adhere to the policies and requirements set forth in this document.

Authority (2.2)

The State Government's Office for Information Resources (OIR) shall have the right to establish and enforce policy and statewide standards as they are related to information security. These policies and standards include, but are not limited to, network and Internet access, any computing platform attached to the State's enterprise network and any wired or wireless technology attached to the State's enterprise network. The Office for Information Resources is responsible and authorized by the State Government to perform audits on any device that attaches to the State Government's enterprise network.

Exceptions (2.3)

All exceptions to any of the security policies shall be reviewed by the Security Advisory Council (SAC) and approved by the Chief Information Security Officer. The exception request process and form can be found in the appendix of this document.

Review (2.4)

Review of this document takes place within the Security Advisory Council sessions and will occur on a semi-annual basis at a minimum. Document review can also be requested by sending a request to the OIR Security Management Team.

Document Format (2.5)

This document generally follows the International Standards Organization (ISO) 17799 standard framework for information technology security management. Each section starts with a high-level policy statement for the domain that is discussed in that section. The high-level policy statement is followed by the objectives of the section. More detailed or specific policy statements follow the objectives. The MINIMUM COMPLIANCE REQUIREMENTS category contains the minimum requirements for compliance criteria that are global and apply to all systems or platforms across the entire enterprise. Finally, the section closes with a description of responsibilities for the Office for Information Resources, agencies and individuals.

X. Section Name

High-level policy statement for section

OBJECTIVES:

Policy Name (x.x)

Policy statement.

Sub-Policy Name (x.x.x)

Sub-policy statement.

Policy Name (x.x)

Policy statement.

Policy Maintenance (2.6)

All policies will be maintained in accordance with the OIR policy process documentation. See the Security Policy Development and Implementation Process located in the appendix of this document.

3. GENERAL INFORMATION SECURITY POLICY

All information resources and information systems owned by the State Government shall be protected from unauthorized disclosure, use, modification or destruction in a manner consistent with their value, sensitivity and criticality to the business and operation of the state government and those it serves. The State Government shall institute an information security program to define the overall information security policy and direction.

OBJECTIVES:

- Ensure that the State Government's information resources are adequately and appropriately protected against unavailability, unauthorized access, modification, destruction or disclosure as required by the Information Systems Council of the State Government.

- Ensure that the State Government provisions an information security program to uphold the State Government's information security requirements.

- Ensure that authorized access to the State Government's information resources is appropriately provisioned.

- Prevent disruption of business processes or service delivery caused by information security inadequacies.

- Ensure that the information security posture of the State Government is appropriately, efficiently and effectively communicated to the stakeholders of the State Government.

- Define and assign responsibilities for protecting information technology resources.

RESPONSIBILITIES:

Office of Information Resources (OIR)

OIR is responsible for establishing and maintaining a statewide information security policy and security program. OIR will ensure that any information processing system attached to the State Government's enterprise network and managed by OIR, or on behalf of OIR, is compliant with this policy document. OIR will ensure that this policy document and any subsequent additions, changes or deletions are communicated appropriately to all agencies of State government.

Agency

Agencies are responsible for ensuring that any information processing system attached to the State Government's enterprise network and managed by the agency, or on behalf of the agency, is compliant with this policy document. Agencies are responsible for developing and implementing procedures and operations processes that support the goals and objectives of this policy document. Agencies may develop agency-specific policy documents provided the minimum requirements set forth in this document are met. Agencies are responsible for communicating this policy document throughout the agency.

Users

Users are responsible for adhering to statewide and agency policies, standards, procedures and guidelines pertaining to information security. For Public Release

4. ORGANIZATIONAL SECURITY POLICY

The State Government shall maintain an organization within the Office for Information Resources (OIR) that is directly responsible for the direction and strategy of the information security program within the State Government and for all agencies of the state government. This group shall be led by the Chief Information Security Officer (CISO) who is ultimately responsible for the direction of the program and for reporting on the State's security posture to the Chief Information Officer (CIO) of the State Government. Each state agency shall appoint an information security "point of contact" (POC).

OBJECTIVES:

- Ensure that the State Government provisions an information security organization, led by a Chief Information Security Officer, to support the State Government's information security requirements.

- Ensure that the information security program can adequately address the requirements set forth by the Information Systems Council.

- Ensure that the State Government provisions an information Security Incident Response Team with appropriate resources to exercise the State Government's information security incident response plan when appropriate.

- Ensure that agencies designate a knowledgeable information security "point of contact" (POC), in accordance with the State Government's "Information Resource Policies" requirements. This POC will act as the central communications figure regarding information security within the agency.

Information Security Infrastructure (4.1)

OIR Security Management shall initiate and control an enterprise information security architecture that includes, but is not limited to, a policy framework, an organizational and communication framework and a security technology framework.

Incident Response Policy (4.2)

The State Government shall establish an information Security Incident Response Team (SIRT). The SIRT will ensure that the State Government can efficiently and effectively communicate information security incidents to the proper stakeholders and respondents of the State. The SIRT members will be appointed based on their position and capabilities within the organization. Each agency shall designate an information security "point of contact" (POC), in accordance with the Information Systems Council's "Information Resource Policies" requirements. This POC will act as the central communications figure regarding security incidents within the agency. The POC shall have responsibility for incident escalations, actions and authority for the administrative oversight of security for the information technology resources under the agency's control. The POC within each agency will participate as a member of the SIRT. The CISO of the State Government will appoint members from within OIR to participate in the SIRT.

Incident Response Plan (4.3)

See the appendix of this document.

RESPONSIBILITIES:

Office of Information Resources (OIR)

OIR is responsible for the establishment of the information security organization as well as the appointment of a Chief Information Security Officer (CISO). The CISO is responsible for the fostering, leadership and communication of the State Government's enterprise security program. The CISO shall establish a Security Advisory Council (SAC). As Chair of the Security Advisory Council (SAC), the CISO will ensure that the proper representatives are appointed to the SAC and will lead the SAC's efforts to develop, implement and maintain an information security program for the State Government. The CISO will chair the SIRT and ensure that it will be appropriately staffed and provisioned, organized, maintained, and will include a representative from each agency. The CISO will also ensure that an information security response plan is developed, maintained, and distributed to all agencies.

Agency

Agencies are responsible for appointing an information security POC. In accordance with ISC policies, the agency POC will have the responsibility and authority for the administrative oversight of security for information resources under the agency's control. The POC shall be available to work with the SIRT and knowledgeable of the information incident response plan. Further, agencies will ensure that the agency POC participates in the "State Government Agency Security Advisory Group" chaired by the CISO.

Users

Users are responsible for reporting suspected or known security violations to the agency's POC and for following instructions pertaining to specific incidents as provided by SIRT members.

5. ASSET CLASSIFICATION AND CONTROL POLICY

All information resource assets owned by the State Government shall be classified in accordance with the requirements set forth within this section in order to ensure that they receive an appropriate level of protection from unauthorized disclosure, use, modification or destruction. Classified assets shall be protected in a manner consistent with their value, sensitivity and criticality to the business and operation of the state government and those it serves or as specified by any superseding State or Federal law or regulation.

Accountability of Assets (5.1)

All information resource assets owned by the State Government shall be accounted for and have a designated custodian. Custodians shall be identified for all information resource assets by each State agency, and the responsibility for the maintenance of appropriate controls, or stewardship, shall be assigned for the assets under the agency's control. Accountability shall remain with the designated custodian of the asset.

Data Classification (5.2)

Data stored or transferred by information resource assets owned by the State Government shall be classified according to the definition of "Personal Information" or "Confidential Records" as specified by applicable State and/or Federal law and regulations to indicate the need, priorities and degree of protection it will receive. At a minimum data shall be classified as public or confidential.

Refer to the State Government Data Classification Standards in Section 6.12.

Public Data Classification Control (5.2.1)

Data classified as public shall be protected from unauthorized modification or destruction.

Refer to the State Government Data Classification Standards in Section 6.12.

Confidential Data Classification Control (5.2.2)

Data classified as confidential shall be protected from unauthorized disclosure, use, modification or destruction.

Refer to the State Government Data Classification Standards in Section 6.12.

RESPONSIBILITIES:

Office of Information Resources

OIR is responsible for the development and maintenance of the statewide information resources asset classification requirements. OIR shall identify asset custodians for the information resources under their direct control. OIR asset custodians shall classify the assets under their control at the time the assets are assigned or created. Asset classification and maintenance can be delegated to an asset steward supervised by the asset custodian. For Public Release

Agency

Agencies are responsible for identifying asset custodians for the resources under their direct control. Agency asset custodians shall classify the assets under their direct control at the time the assets are assigned or created. Asset classification and maintenance can be delegated to an asset steward supervised by the asset custodian.

Users

Users shall responsibly work with the assets they are assigned and due care shall be taken to protect any mobile computing asset from theft or destruction. Users shall not provide access to information resource assets without obtaining authorization from the asset custodian. For Public Release

6. PERSONNEL SECURITY POLICY

Personnel Background Investigation (6.1)

Current Gap

Acceptable Use Policy (6.2)

Refer to Attachment 6.10 – State Government Acceptable Use Policy

7. PHYSICAL AND ENVIRONMENTAL SECURITY POLICY

Physical access to the State Government's information resource assets and infrastructure will be restricted to individuals who require that access to perform their job function.

OBJECTIVES:

- To prevent unauthorized access, damage or interference to State Government premises and information.

- To prevent loss, damage or compromise of processing equipment or network components.

Secure Areas (7.1)

Critical/sensitive business information processing facilities shall be housed in secure areas, protected by a defined security perimeter, with appropriate security barriers and entry controls that protect them from unauthorized access, damage and/or interference.

Physical Security Perimeter (7.1.1)

All critical/sensitive enterprise processing facilities shall have multiple layers of physical security. Each layer shall be independent and separate of the preceding and/or following layer(s).

All other processing facilities shall have, at a minimum, a single security perimeter protecting it from unauthorized access, damage and/or interference.

Equipment Security (7.2)

Processing equipment shall be sited or protected to reduce the risks from environmental threats and hazards, and to reduce the opportunities for unauthorized access.

Equipment Placement and Protection (7.2.1)

Equipment shall be located in secured areas. Equipment located in areas where the State Government is unable to maintain a secure perimeter shall be locked in a secured cabinet with access controlled by the State Government. Secured cabinets or facilities shall support further segregation within the State Government's Information Technology (IT) organization based on role and responsibility.

Power Supplies (7.2.2)

Infrastructure and related computing equipment shall be protected from power failures and other electrical anomalies.

Cabling Security (7.2.3)

Power and telecommunications cabling carrying data or supporting information services shall be protected from unauthorized interception or damage.

General Security Controls (7.3)

Information shall be protected from disclosure to, modification or theft by unauthorized persons.

Clear Screen Policy (7.3.1)

All endpoints that provide access to Information Processing Systems shall be configured so that a screen-saver, with password protection engaged, or other lock-down mechanism that prevents unauthorized viewing of screen information or unauthorized access to the system shall automatically be implemented if the system has been left unattended.

All computing platforms with attached displays shall be oriented away from direct line of sight from unauthorized viewers.

RESPONSIBILITIES:

Office of Information Resources (OIR)

OIR is responsible for developing requirements and guidelines for physical access to enterprise information resource assets and infrastructure. OIR will ensure that appropriate protective mechanisms are installed to restrict access to the enterprise information resource assets and infrastructure, in coordination with appropriate departments. Further, OIR will ensure physical access to enterprise assets is monitored, and unauthorized access is reported to management or the proper authorities.

Agency

Agencies are responsible for implementing practices and procedures and installing protective mechanisms to ensure local information assets are protected from unauthorized access. Agencies are also responsible for ensuring that physical access to agency hosted assets is monitored and that unauthorized access is reported to management or the proper authorities.

Users

Users should report any suspicious activity or persons to management or the proper authorities. Users should also refrain from behaviors that could compromise the physical protection of information technology resources such as willful assistance without proper identification, tailgating through doors or sharing facility access keys or codes. For Public Release

8. COMMUNICATIONS AND OPERATIONS MANAGEMENT POLICY

All agencies of the State Government shall document and maintain standard security operating procedures and configurations for their respective operating environments.

OBJECTIVES:

- Reduce the risk of liability for the unauthorized usage of unlicensed software and minimize the threat of exposure due to software weaknesses and/or configurations.

- Prevent the automated propagation of malicious code and contamination of sterile environments attached to the enterprise network.

- Ensure that media resources containing sensitive data are sanitized before transferal or reuse and that they are destroyed when decommissioned and not selected for reuse or transfer.

- Protect critical state information resource assets, including hardware, software and data from unauthorized use, misuse, or destruction.

Operational Procedures and Responsibilities (8.1)

The operating procedures identified by the security policy shall be documented and maintained by the appropriate process owners.

Documentation of Operating Procedures (8.1.1)

Operating procedures relating to security shall be treated as formal documents and changes shall be authorized by management.

Operational Change Control (8.1.2)

Changes to information processing facilities and systems shall be controlled and monitored for security compliance. Formal management responsibilities and procedures shall exist to ensure satisfactory control of all changes to equipment, software, configurations or procedures that affect the security of the State Government's operational environment.

All written documentation generated by the change control policies shall be retained as evidence of compliance.

Segmentation and Layered Security (8.1.3)

The State Government's operational environment shall support segmentation and layered security technologies and configurations based on role, risk, sensitivity, and access control rules.

Segregation of Duties (8.1.4)

Current Gap

Separation of Development and Production Facilities (8.1.5)

Current Gap

Production Environment Access Control (8.1.6)

Current Gap

System Planning and Acceptance (8.2)

Current Gap

System Acceptance (8.2.1)

Current Gap

Capacity Planning (8.3)

Current Gap

Software Control (8.4)

All software installed within the State's operational environment shall support security mechanisms that provide data integrity, confidentiality and availability. Software shall support security event monitoring and audit ability.

Authorized and Licensed Software (8.4.1)

Only licensed software procured through State Government contracts or software acquired with Office for Information Resources (OIR) involvement in the procurement process shall be installed in the State's environment. Software that does not require a purchase (i.e. General Public License, FreeWare, ShareWare) shall be approved as a State standard software product through the State's architecture standards approval process.

Malicious Software Control (8.4.2)

All computing platforms that are attached to the State's enterprise technology infrastructure shall be protected from intentional or unintentional exposure to malicious software. Malicious software includes, but is not limited to, software viruses, worms, Trojan horses and/or logic bombs.

Compromised System Policy (8.4.2.1)

Any system found infected with "Rootkit" malicious software is considered fully compromised. Fully compromised systems shall be removed from the operational environment. OIR Security Management reserves the right to seize any compromised system for forensic analysis.

Patch Management Control (8.4.3)

All applications and processing devices that are attached to the State's enterprise technology infrastructure shall be kept up to date with security related patches made available by the software or hardware vendor.

Media Handling and Security (8.4.4)

Software licensed to the State Government shall be installed only on systems or devices covered by the license agreement.

Application Control (8.4.5)

Current Gap

Media Disposal and Reuse (8.5)

All data storage devices (media) subject to transfer or reuse must be sanitized in accordance with the State Government's media reuse procedure or superseding State or Federal requirements. Media assets that are not subject to transfer or reuse must be destroyed in accordance with the State Government's media disposal procedures or in accordance with superseding State or Federal requirements.

RESPONSIBILITIES:

Office of Information Resources

OIR is responsible for maintaining network infrastructure and enterprise component software and operating system configurations with the latest release of security related updates compatible with the State's enterprise environment and will provide a means by which authentic, tested and approved security related software updates can be deployed and implemented by agencies across the enterprise. OIR will deploy and monitor security control devices to facilitate a means by which all processing devices attached to the enterprise network environment can be protected from intentional or unintentional exposure to malicious software. OIR will establish, maintain, and follow procedures to prevent the propagation of malicious code and/or system abuse. OIR will develop and maintain supporting guidelines and documentation and will ensure that contracts for standard software products and media destruction services are maintained. Finally, OIR will work with vendors/contractors (engaged through OIR) and who are responsible for non-state managed devices to ensure they understand and comply with these responsibilities.

Agency

Agencies will establish agency policy and procedures for media disposal or reuse, including personally and/or contractor owned devices, and will ensure that any agency media disposal and reuse procedure complies with superseding State or Federal sanitizing requirements that may be specific for the agency. Agencies systems attached to the State Government's enterprise network will participate in enterprise patch management and malicious software control programs. Agencies will be responsible for testing patches prior to release in the agency's environment. Agencies will also ensure that all systems not able to participate in an automatic security related update process are kept up to date through an additional manual process. This process, along with the participating systems, must be documented and made available for periodic audit by the OIR Security Management Team. Agencies will utilize software products that have been approved as standard for the State Government. Finally, agencies will ensure vendors/contractors (engaged through the agency) who are responsible for non-state-managed devices understand and comply with these responsibilities.

Users

Users are responsible for ensuring that devices assigned to them retain the ability to participate in automatic security software update environments (i.e. Disabling automatic enterprise configurations is prohibited). Users are to only utilize software products that have been approved as standard for the State Government, and they are to abstain from downloading unauthorized software or installing personally owned software.

9. ACCESS CONTROL POLICY

Access to the State Government's information resources shall be granted consistent with the concept of least privilege. All information processing systems owned by the State Government shall have an appropriate role-based access control system that ensures only legitimate users and/or systems have access to data resources that they are explicitly authorized to use. All information processing systems shall have the capability to interact with the statewide access control environment. Access to any State Government information processing system is generally forbidden unless explicitly permitted.

OBJECTIVES:

- Ensure that authorized access to the State Government's information resources is appropriately provisioned.

- Ensure that unauthorized access to information resources is appropriately prevented.

- Minimize information technology risks through the use of access control methodologies and techniques.

- Ensure that a means to segment and control enterprise network traffic is implemented.

- Ensure that all interconnectivity between the State Government's enterprise network and any other network is provisioned securely.

Access Control Rules (9.1)

Access control rules and requirements to access the State Government's information resources shall be developed, documented and maintained by their respective resource owners. All agency specific-access control rules and requirements must be made available for audit by the Office for Information Resources (OIR) Security Management Team and in compliance with the State Government enterprise security policies. All enterprise access control rules and requirements must be approved by the OIR Security Management Team.

User Access Management (9.2)

All State Government agencies shall develop, document and maintain user access and account management procedures. These procedures shall include, but are not limited to, new account provisioning, account transfer and/or job profile changes and account termination and/or de-provisioning.

User Registration and Authorization (9.2.1)

Current Gap

Loss of User Privilege (9.2.1.1)

Current Gap

User Privilege Control (9.2.2)

Current Gap

User Identification and Authorization (9.2.3)

At a minimum, user access to protected information resources requires the utilization of User Identification (UserID) and password that uniquely identifies the user. Sharing access credentials intended to authenticate and authorize a single user between any two or more individuals is prohibited.

User Account Lockout (9.2.4)

Limits shall be set for the number of unsuccessful logins that can be attempted for a UserID.

User Password Management (9.2.5)

Passwords assigned to users must be created and managed to protect against unauthorized discovery or usage and must meet the minimum password requirements.

Review of User Access Rights (9.2.6)

Current Gap

Network Access Control (9.3)

The State Government's enterprise network shall be designed to provide the ability to segregate and control traffic between systems, connected devices and third party environments based on role, risk and sensitivity. The enterprise network will allow for specific services at all seven layers of the Open Systems Interconnection (OSI) model to be made available or filtered, depending on legitimate business need. All access and connectivity to the State Government's enterprise network must comply with the State Government's security requirements for enterprise network interconnectivity. All access and connectivity to the State Government's enterprise network shall be granted consistent with the concept of least privilege. Access and connectivity to the State Government's enterprise network is generally forbidden unless explicitly permitted.

User Authentication for Network Connections (9.3.1)

Current Gap

Segregation in Networks (9.3.2)

All enterprise network architectures operated by, or on behalf of, the State Government shall be designed to support, at a minimum, separate public, "demilitarized" and private security zones based on role, risk and sensitivity. Bridging between separate security zones is strictly prohibited. All access between separate security zones shall be controlled by a security mechanism configured to deny all access by default unless explicitly authorized and approved by the OIR Security Management Team.

Enterprise Interconnectivity Requirements (9.3.3)

All systems attached to the State Government's enterprise network shall comply with the security requirements for enterprise interconnectivity documentation.

Operating System Access Control (9.4)

Current Gap

Session Time Outs (9.4.1)

Current Gap

Password Management System (9.4.2)

Current Gap

Use of Shared Technology Resources (9.4.3)

Current Gap

Logon Banner (9.4.4)

All systems and devices owned and operated by or on behalf of the State Government must display the State approved logon banner before the user logs in.

Mobile and Workstation Computing (9.5)

All mobile and workstation computing platforms, including but not limited to desktops, laptops, hand-held devices, and portable storage media, shall be protected from unauthorized use, modification or destruction. Mobile and workstation computing platform capabilities shall be granted to individuals or entities that require such access and facilities to perform their specific job related duties. Confidential data assets shall not be stored on mobile and/or workstation computing platforms unless absolutely necessary.

Mobile Computing Policy (9.5.1)

Mobile computing platforms shall be physically protected against theft when left unattended. Mobile computing platforms shall not store confidential data assets where it is not absolutely necessary to perform the specific job related duties. Storage of confidential data assets on a mobile computing platform must have approval from the asset custodian for such storage. Confidential data assets which have been authorized for mobile use must be encrypted while stored on mobile computing platforms.

Workstation Computing Policy (9.5.2)

Workstation computing platforms shall be physically protected against theft when left unattended. Workstation computing platforms shall not store confidential data assets where it is not absolutely necessary to perform the specific job related duties. Storage of confidential data assets on a workstation computing platform must have approval from the asset custodian for such storage. Confidential data assets which have been authorized to be stored on the local workstation must be encrypted while stored on the workstation computing platform.

Monitoring System Access and Use (9.6)

Current Gap

Event Logging (9.6.1)

Current Gap

Clock Synchronization (9.6.2)

Current Gap

RESPONSIBILITIES:

Office of Information Resources (OIR)

OIR will ensure that all enterprise networks are provisioned and segmented with the appropriate levels of security in regards to role, risk and sensitivity. They will also develop, implement and maintain guidelines for password management and maintenance. OIR will ensure that all third parties are aware of and compliant with the State Government's Third Party Connectivity Agreement prior to the establishment of the interconnection. OIR is responsible for the management and processing of granting or rejecting third party interconnectivity requests. OIR shall ensure that due diligence and care is taken to fulfill any protection requirements of the mobile computing platforms for which OIR is responsible.

Agency

Agencies are responsible for implementing a process for identifying and documenting legitimate "need" for users to have access to the State Government's information resources. This process will include review and revalidation of existing users. Agencies will ensure that all requirements of a third party network connection to the State Government's enterprise network are presented to the OIR Security Management Team for review, approval or rejection prior to implementing the connection. Agencies shall ensure that due diligence and care is taken to fulfill any protection requirements of the mobile computing platforms for which each agency is responsible.

Users

Individual users are uniquely identified by their respective access credentials and are responsible for maintaining the confidentiality of those credentials. Users should refrain from using authentication credentials intended for the protection of State Government assets on personal computing platforms or non-State related websites. For Public Release

10. SYSTEMS DEVELOPMENT AND MAINTENANCE POLICY

Systems Development and Maintenance Control Policy 10.0

Current Gap

11. COMPLIANCE POLICY

All State Government agencies must be compliant with this security policy document

Compliance with Legal Requirements (11.1)

All State Government agencies must be compliant with any State or Federal regulatory requirements which supersede this policy document.

Applicable Legislation (11.1.1)

All State Government agencies must be compliant with any legislation enacted by the State Government in regards to the management of information resources on behalf of the State.

Data Protection and Privacy (11.1.2)

All State Government agency data custodians must ensure that all "Personal Information" data assets, as defined by applicable State and/or Federal law and regulations, are protected from unauthorized use, modification or disclosure.

Data Breach and Disclosure (11.1.3)

Any State Government agency that discovers a breach of the information security controls set forth in this document which results in disclosure of unencrypted "personal information" about persons to unauthorized third parties shall provide notice of the disclosure in accordance with State law, mandates, and acts.

Internal Compliance Matrix (11.2)

See the Appendix of this document for the policy compliance matrix, which indicates the dates by which all agencies must be compliant with the relative policy components. Those agencies that cannot meet the compliance deadline must file for an exception using the security policy exception process.

12. BUSINESS CONTINUITY MANAGEMENT POLICY

While Business Continuity Management is included in the International Standards Organization (ISO) 17799 standards, it is outside the scope of the security organization within OIR, but it is within the scope of this RFP.

Agencies are expected to collaborate with the State's administrative services agencies to ensure their ability to recover from any disaster and to maintain business operations including an agency business impact analysis (BIA), business continuity plan (BCP), and disaster recovery plan (DRP).